Marriage and Sacrament:
A Theology of Christian Marriage

Michael G. Lawler

A Michael Glazier Book
THE LITURGICAL PRESS
Collegeville, Minnesota

A Michael Glazier Book published by The Liturgical Press

Cover design by Greg Becker

	2	3	4	5	6	7	8	9

Library of Congress Cataloging-in-Publication Data

Lawler, Michael G.
    Marriage and sacrament : a theology of Christian marriage / by Michael G. Lawler.
        p.   cm.
    "A Michael Glazier book."
    Includes bibliographical references.
    ISBN 0-8146-5051-1
    1. Marriage—Religious aspects—Catholic Church.   2. Catholic Church—Doctrines   I. Title.
BX2250.L369   1993
234'.165—dc20   93-22619
                                                                 CIP

For Will and Willma
with whom the future of marriage and sacrament rests

Contents

Abbreviations

AAS	*Acta Apostolicae Sedis* (Roma: Typis Polyglottis Vaticanis)
DS	*Enchiridion Symbolorum Definitionum et Declarationum de Rebus Fidei et Morum,* H. Denzinger and A. Schoenmetzer, eds. (Freiburg: Herder, 1965)
DV	*Dei Verbum* (Dogmatic Constitution on Divine Revelation), *The Documents of Vatican II,* Walter M. Abbott, ed.
GS	*Gaudium et Spes* (Pastoral Constitution on the Church in the Modern World), *The Documents of Vatican II,* Walter M. Abbott, ed.
LG	*Lumen Gentium* (Dogmatic Constitution on the Church), *The Documents of Vatican II,* Walter M. Abbott, ed.
PG	*Patrologiae Cursus Completus: Series Graeca,* J. P. Migne, ed.
PL	*Patrologiae Cursus Completus: Series Latina,* J. P. Migne, ed.
ST	*Summa Theologiae Sancti Thomae de Aquino*
TS	*Theological Studies* (Georgetown University)

All abbreviations throughout the book are listed without any underlined emphasis. All translations from languages other than English are the author's.

Introduction

In the contemporary western world, marriage is under fire from two different directions. On one side, there are those who bemoan the passing of the traditional, patriarchal family with its clear role assignments and structures of authority. On the other side, there are those who denigrate the marital structures of permanence and exclusivity which continue to persist. Both sides claim, though for different reasons, that marriage is on the wane or, at the very least, in deep crisis. This book grows out of my belief that the first claim is demonstrably nonsense and the second demonstrably correct. It seeks to speak to the crisis in marriage, specifically to the crisis in the understanding of sacramental marriage or marriage in the Lord.

The social sciences, which expend great energy on such matters, provide no support for the claim that marriage is on the wane. Women and men continue to marry today at about the same rate as they married a century ago. Many, indeed, marry two or three times, a fact which indicates some crisis or need for judgment. My judgment is that the crisis arises, at least in part, from a cultural change in the understanding of marriage, specifically in the understanding of spousal roles.

An ancient definition of marriage is found in the *Instituta* of the Roman Emperor Justinian (1,9,1): "Marriage is a union of a man and a woman, embracing an undivided communion of life." Though this so-called definition is no more than a description of how marriage was lived in the empire, it has exercised tight control over subsequent discussions about the nature of marriage in the western world. It recurs, for instance, in the definition of marriage advanced by the Second Vatican Council: marriage is, "an intimate partnership of marital life and love" (GS 48). Definitions, of course, however clear they seek to be or appear to be, are always in need of interpretation, and this one is no different. In the classical days of marriage theory, the union and communion that is marriage was interpreted as an *unequal* partnership, the husband being the major and authoritative partner, the wife a minor and frequently silent partner. It is precisely in this interpretive, cultural process, and specifically in its outcomes, that there has been a change in marriage theory. It is precisely this change that has, at least in part, driven marriage into crisis in the West.

You will meet in this book a young man named Will and a young woman named Willma who, though fictionalized, are real indeed. Will and Willma have fallen in love and have decided to get married so that they may spend the rest of their lives together in an *equal* partnership, one that is equally beneficial to both of them. Neither invented such an expectation for marriage; they learned it in the culture in which they grew up and in which the expectation of equal partnership has become dominant.

That marriage is an equal partnership is not the only thing that Will and Willma have learned from their culture. They have learned also that marriage, like life, may be described in the metaphor of the journey. "We want to journey together through life," they told me, "but as equal wife and husband." This metaphor of equal partnership on the journey of life and marriage entails demands upon the spouses quite different from the classical metaphor of marriage as stable institution. In the stable institution, spousal roles are clear and consistently enforced across the culture. The journey is anything but stable and clear; it can throw up the unexpected at any moment. The journey metaphor blurs the clarity and consequent rigidity of the institution metaphor.

The reader needs to know one more thing about Will and Willma. They are not only two young people about to be married, but also two believing Catholics about to be married. Like them, and the culture in which they grew up, the church to which they belong has recently rediscovered the metaphor of the journey. The nineteenth century Church was imaged, as much as marriage, as stable institution, maybe more so since this Church was assumed to have continued unchanged and unchanging since its foundation by Jesus. That image, and all that it entailed, was found to be historically inaccurate, and was displaced at the Second Vatican Council by the biblical image of the "pilgrim church" (LG 48–51), an exodus Church on a journey through the desert of history to a promised paradise. As it changed its metaphors for itself the Church also changed its metaphors for marriage, from metaphor of stable biological structure and consequent functions, to metaphor of changing personal relationships. That change of metaphors occasioned a crisis, that is, a time of judgment for marriage, for it occasioned a time of judgment for spouses.

The popular perception is that more marriages end in divorce today than at any other time in history. The social sciences demonstrate that perception is inaccurate, almost hysterical. The fact is there has been only the slightest uprise in the rate of divorce today from the rate in the nineteenth century, and the uprise is abating. The further fact, however, is that all of us have somehow been personally touched by divorce, at work or in our neighborhood or in our family; and as Will and Willma contemplate marriage, they fear divorce. They know they love one another, but they also know others who have loved one another just as much and whose marriages ended in divorce. They know they want their marriage to last as long as their lives last, but they also know that those who fall in love can also fall out of love. They ask what they can do to ensure that they do not fall out of love, that their marriage does not end, that they remain best friends forever. This book offers them one closely examined way to reach their marital goals, the way of religious faith and hope and love, the way of sacrament.

Since the fourth-century and Augustine, the Catholic Church has insisted that there is a sacrament in marriage between Christians. Since the thirteenth-century and Aquinas, it has insisted that a marriage between Christians is as much sacrament as the great sacraments of baptism and eucharist. Gradually, it has come to insist specifically that it is the marital relationship between the spouses that is the sacrament. This book is offered to Will and Willma, and to all those Christians who are married, as an extended analysis of the sacrament of marriage and of the contribution it can make to achieving the goal of an equal partnership of love until death parts them. The book examines the relationships between friendship, love, marriage and the sacrament (chapter 1), the Christian meanings of the sacrament (chapter 2), the biblical basis of the sacrament (chapter 3), the varied history of the sacrament (chapter 4), the tragedy of the ending of marriage and sacrament (chapter 5), and finally some crucial questions related to Will and Willma's desire that their marriage should be mutually and equally fruitful and should last as long as life lasts (chapter 6). As a married theologian in the Catholic tradition, I offer this book to them, and to all those who are married, and to the Church, as a positive and constructive interpretation and contemporary articulation of the Catholic tradition concerning marriage and sacrament.

I repeat again here what I have said several times before. No author writes a book in isolation; he is subject to multiple influences. I am happy to confess that I am no exception to that rule, and I freely express my gratitude to all those teachers, colleagues, students and friends with whom I have dialogued over the years, and from whom I have learned what marriage means in the Catholic tradition. Since I cannot name all of them, it seems churlish to name any of them. I name only Will and Willma, to whom this book is dedicated. For the future of marriage and sacrament rests now with them and their generation.

1

Marriage and the Sacrament of Marriage

This opening chapter is ultimately about two realities, marriage and the sacrament of marriage. Before we can begin to understand these realities, however, we must first understand two other common human realities closely related to them, namely, friendship and love. This chapter, therefore, considers four things: friendship, love, marriage and the sacrament of marriage. We shall deal with each in turn.

Friendship

Even the most egocentric of persons recognizes that he or she cannot survive without other persons. If one doesn't associate with other persons, care for them, assist them, see to their needs, and let them do the same in return, then both will fail to become integrated human beings. Born of a woman, each of us is classified as human, but that names only our physiology. Without other human persons in our lives, without emotional intimacy, intellectual stimulation, personal and social connectedness, we will never achieve full humanity.

No one will let everyone into one's life, because that project is too vast; and not everyone will let one of us into their lives. Those few we do let in and who let us in are, therefore, apart from the general crowd, and are named apart from the crowd. They are named *friends*, without whom, as Aristotle wrote, "no one would choose to live, even if he had all other goods."[1] It is that special thing that friends share, namely, friendship, that is the subject matter of this section.

Friendship is not new in human history. Aristotle is witness to that, and we may begin our search for understanding with him. He distinguishes three kinds of friendship, which he names friendships of pleasure, of usefulness and of good. In the first, some quality in another person, Aristotle mentions wit, affords me pleasure; in the second, the other person is seen as somehow useful to me; in the third, it is the good in the other person, and therefore the other person himself or herself, that I love.

In each of these three friendships, it is some good that is loved, for good is always the object of love. But, in these three, the good is loved differently. When I love someone for the pleasure he or she gives me (and I do not intend exclusively sexual pleasure), then I love primarily something pleasurable to *me*. When I love a person for his or her usefulness to me, then I love something useful to *me*. When I love a person for the goodness that is in that person, and *is* that person, then I love *him* or *her,* not just something pleasant or useful to me. This person's goodness may be, of course, both pleasurable and useful to me, but in the third friendship it is not pleasure or usefulness but the *person* that I love. In Aristotle's judgment, only the third kind of friendship qualifies as true friendship.[2]

All who enjoy or who have enjoyed true friendship will recognize that such friendship requires time, for "it is impossible for men to know one another before they have eaten salt together, nor can they admit each other to intimacy nor become friends before each appears to be worthy of friendship and confidence." To be a perfect friendship, it must also be reciprocal.[3]

Another wise Greek, Plato, agrees that friendship is based on the good in friends. No person, however, he argues in *Lysis*, can be good in everything but only in some things. Lysis, for instance, is good at reading, writing and playing the lyre, not so good at driving a chariot, weaving and household management. Lysis, of course, represents every person, good in a few things, deficient in many. Plato uses this common, and commonly recognized, situation at the end of the dialogue to set forth the principle of friendship, which is a principle of congeniality and reciprocity of goods. Persons need the goods of others different from their own and, therefore, congenial to them. Good persons admire, rather than envy, the good, whether in themselves or in others.[4] This mutual admiration and valuation of personal goods, and of one another, is called friendship.

Rubin lists "the minimum requirements . . . to be counted as a friend." They are "trust, honesty, respect, commitment, safety, support, generosity, loyalty, mutuality, constancy, understanding, acceptance."[5] A short reflection on just two of these qualities will help to concretize and illumine the goods which men and women admire, value and seek in friendship.

The first reflection is on trust, interestingly the first quality Rubin lists. Speaking of trust in the small child, psychiatrist Erik Erikson comments that "consistency, continuity and sameness of experience provide a rudimentary sense of ego identity."[6] Trust, confidence in the integrity and consistency of character of familiar and predictable people, usually parents, is critical to the formation of a positive sense of self in the child. It is critical also to the formation of friendship.

I need someone who can consistently accept and understand me with my foibles and weaknesses and surprises, who can be patient with and sustaining of me, who will not be judgmental and condemnatory. I need someone before whom I can bare my soul, perhaps even my body, someone who can bare both her soul and her body to me. I need someone with whom I can say in tune: "We have known one another a long time; we have come to know everything about one another; we have come to know we can depend on one another. We have earned one another's trust." Both Erikson and Rubin are, I believe, correct. As trust is something children must learn to discover who they are, so also is it something men and women must learn to become friends. Trust is the absolute bedrock of friendship; there is no friendship without it.

The second reflection is on safety or security, from physical dangers, of course, but most especially from ever-threatening emotional dangers, self-doubt, shame, fear, anxiety. I live in a highly competitive world, a world in which I must forever meet established standards and demands—as well as the doubt and the fear that I cannot measure up to them. I need places and times and, above all, persons (friends) with whom I do not need to measure up, with whom I can relax, let my hair down and be myself. The safest place against self-doubt, fear and anxiety about relationships is, it is easy to think, a self-protective cocoon. It is also the most useless and, in the end, most stultifying place, for in that place I will never become humanly actualized. I need a trusted someone (a friend) to bring me out of my womb-cocoon, to hold out expectations for me, to make demands upon me, to point me towards the fulfillment of my modest potential, to rejoice with me when I attain it. I know and feel this of myself, and also of every other woman and man I know.

I know this to be true: if friendships are to survive, they must be kept alive by friends. My friends and I must work unceasingly at our friendships, we must care for them, nurture them, jealously sustain them, for they will not sustain themselves. Many of my friendships, cavalierly projected to be lifelong, have died. I am not sure (or perhaps I am just unwilling to admit) if it was because both of us took for granted a relationship we wanted to keep alive, or if it was because one or other of us did not value our friendship enough to work at it. I know only that many friendships have died over the long-distance years, lending verisimilitude to the saying ascribed to Harry Truman: "You want a friend for life, get a dog!" I know, as a final comment for this section, that Truman's saying is not true. Long-standing, trusted and secure friendships give lie to this cynical assumption. Such friendships, however, are the ones that I, and we, have committed to, have worked at and have sustained. I am confident that every reader can say the same.

Love

The preceding section is easy to summarize. I have needs, and so do others: needs for trust, for honesty, for respect, for safety, for understanding, for encouragement, for acceptance as I am. Some people commit themselves to respond to my needs and I commit myself to respond to theirs. We are, we say, friends. We accompany one another on life's journey; we reveal ourselves mutually to one another; we assist one another and sustain one another when one or the other is weak; we provoke one another to realize our highest potential, to be the best we can be; we rejoice together when the best is achieved. In short, we wish one another well or, in an ancient word, we love one another.[7] It is this love, this wishing each other well, that I seek to clarify in this section.

The question, "what is the meaning of love?", appears simple and straightforward. But any lover can tell you that love is far from simple and straightforward, and so too is the intense debate and the variety of answers the question has generated over the centuries. Each in their different ways testify to the fact that love is complex and mysterious, and that the claim "I love you" is best followed by silence, not by explanation. In this section, I am a man who has said to other women or men, "I love you," and has been immediately asked "what do you mean?" I shall attempt to answer that question in two ways: first abstractly, as a philosopher, and then concretely, as a lover.

Aristotle, we recall, distinguished three kinds of friendship. There is the friendship of pleasure and of usefulness, in which another person is loved as pleasant or useful to me, and there is the friendship of good, in which he or she is loved for himself/herself. Thomas Aquinas makes a similar distinction with respect to love. He distinguishes between *amor concupiscentiae*, the love that is desire, and *amor amicitiae*, the love that is friendship. The two are distinguished to the extent that in the love of desire I desire something, perhaps even someone, as good for *me*, while in the love of friendship I love someone who is good in *himself* or *herself*.[8] I shall call these two loves *desire* and *love* respectively. It is love, in all its charm and mystery, that is intended when I say, "I love *you*," and mean it.

We may begin our search for the meaning of love in a way that will appear strange but that will lead us surely to an important conclusion. We begin with another of Aquinas' distinctions, the distinction between knowing and loving: "Knowledge is of things as they exist in the knower; the will is related to things as they exist in themselves."[9] To know means to receive into oneself; to love means to transcend oneself, to go out of oneself to another. Love, as every lover knows, is essentially ec-static. To know someone is to know her within me; to love her is to love her as *she* is in her own absoluteness apart from me. The distinction underscores an important fact about love. In love, I go *out of myself* to another self like me.

The importance of this discovery about love is already hinted at in Cicero's description of a friend as "a second self."[10] If there is ever to be a second self, however, there must be a first self. For me, that first self is me; for you, it is you. If I am ever to grasp and value and cherish you as a second self, I must first consciously grasp, value and cherish me as a first self. This self is a richness, a powerful center of action, always present but mysterious, always experienced as capable of new revelations, never exhaustively understood. It is this first self I love when I love myself; it is a similar, but distinctively unique, self I love when I love you.

This realization of the self-based character of love leads us forward to a further discovery. "You shall love your neighbor as yourself," the Gospel says (Matt 22:39). Just what we have talking about, I hear you say. Not quite, I respond, at least not until the full story is told. Both Aristotle and Aquinas insist that friendship happens, not when I love another as myself but only when my love is reciprocated. "Friendship requires mutual love, because a friend is a friend to a friend."[11] Anyone who has ever loved another "from afar" knows that. Friendship is never one-sided; there is no real friendship, no real love, until love is reciprocated by the beloved. This mutual love between two equal selves, between a distinct "I" and a distinct "Thou," creates between them the intimate communion that is the distinguishing characteristic of lovers. A commentary on that communion will conclude the philosophical part of this section.

Webster derives *communion* from the Latin *communis*, common, and defines it as common sharing, common possession, common ownership. We could add common responsibility and, in the matter that concerns us here, namely, the communion between lovers, common creation and ongoing animation by love. A frequent problem comes into focus here. In the loving communion between an I and a Thou, in which each loves the other *self*, communion cannot mean fusion of the two selves, it cannot mean identification of one of the lovers with the other. An element of *otherness* is central to the communion that arises from and is sustained by love. I love, not *my*-self (though self-love is involved) but an-*other* self, "a unique and free initiative who in his uniqueness is turned towards me and . . . reveals somehow that hidden treasure which is himself."[12]

The communion between lovers has no obvious models in our world other than itself. It is certainly not a monarchy, which emphasizes unequal individuals. It is not even a democracy, which emphasizes equal but separate individuals. Without models, all I can say is that it is a communion, in which a unique I and a unique Thou become an organic We, lovingly sharing in common their thoughts, their feelings, their dreams, their possessions and, on occasion, even their bodies. The well-known biblical aphorism about a husband and a wife becoming "one body" (Gen 2:24) creates a paradoxical problem here, because it is better known than understood. I shall return to it later in some detail. For the moment, I note only that it is never to be interpreted as meaning that the persons in the communion that is love merge their selves into one or the other. Such submergence and loss of self-identity sometimes happens in relationships, but it happens always with the loss, not only of identity, but also of love and communion. Admired, valued and cherished otherness is integral to the relationship that is true love.

We have now reached the stage of our inquiry when the philosopher must fall silent to let the lover explain in more concrete language. Two phrases in our language sum up everything I have been saying in the preceding analysis. The first is "falling in love," the second is "being in love." It is time to confront the concrete reality lying behind these phrases, and I shall do so in the time-honored way, by telling a not-so-fictionalized story.

A young man and a young woman, Will and Willma respectively, are approaching emotional maturity. Each has developed a rather positive sense of self and self-worth; each is more self-directed than earlier in life. Both, as the common saying has it, know who they are; they no longer merely follow the crowd. They meet.

Will has fallen in love before, three times in fact, once when he was sixteen, once when he was nineteen and again when he was twenty three. Each time had ended in disappointment, especially the most recent occurrence when he had been sure that, in Cindy, he had found the perfect woman for him. He had opened more of his private self to Cindy, invested more of his emotional energy in his relationship with her, even mortgaged his dreamed-of future to her, and Cindy had betrayed his trust and violated their friendship. Will's disappointment and pain were great, almost unbearable, and he vowed "never again." Never again will I permit myself to be so vulnerable; never again will I allow another to make such a fool of me. His friends noticed a change in him. He became more withdrawn, less communicative, more distant, more cynical and calculating. When he met Willma, it did not take him long to realize he was falling in love again.

Willma, he admitted to himself and to his friends, was not exactly a "looker", though she was not ugly either. He couldn't exactly say why he was drawn to her; there was just something, chemistry was all he could call it. He was drawn out of himself, out of his self-protective cocoon, to commune with this very feminine person. He liked the tender way she touched him, both emotionally and physically; he liked the way she was sensitive to his needs; he liked the way she could read his moods; he liked the way she dealt with him as an equal, asking his suggestions on this and that, offering suggestions of her own; he liked the growing reciprocity between them.

Will soon had a choice to make and so, too, did Willma. What about his "never again" resolution? Would he hold to it, keep himself to himself, or would he give himself again, let himself love and be loved by this enchanting woman? When he decided to let himself go and to reciprocate Willma's willing love, he just knew that he wanted their friendship, their love, their communion to extend to the very depth of their separate selves and to be forever. Though he did not know it yet, for he had not known Willma nearly long enough, and he had been deceived three times before, he wanted them to be best friends forever. He was ready for that ritualizing of commitment to friendship and love called marriage and so also, in this account, was Willma, who reciprocated everything he felt. So, too, are we ready to speak about marriage.

Marriage

Every reader of this book has been to a wedding. It may have been a civil wedding presided over by a judge; it may have been a religious wedding presided over by a minister. It has always been a solemn, joyous, celebratory occasion. For a valid marriage, however, only one moment of the ritual truly counts, the solemn moment of giving consent. At the wedding of Will and Willma, those gathered hang breathlessly on these, or similar, solemn words. "I, Will, take you, Willma, for my lawful wife, to have and to hold, from this day forward, for better, for worse, for richer, for poorer, in sickness and in health, until death do us part." When Willma declares her intention in the same words, you hear them pronounced wedded, married, "husband and wife." If that moment of free consent is missing or in any way flawed, there is no wedding and there is no marriage. I shall return to this in a moment.

The fact that friendship and love die over the years is immortalized in the great love stories of our culture: Tristan and Isolde, Romeo and Juliet, even "Love Story." That marriages die is immortalized in the more mundane statistics of our divorce courts; they tell us that some forty per cent die in the United States. Important though love and marriage may be to Will and Willma, marriage is even more important to the society in which they live, because it is still the ordinary way to provide good citizens for the society. The societal stake in marriage so outweighs in importance the individual commitment to it that every society has prescribed for marriage the solemn ritualization of commitment. It is this public, ritual commitment that makes married love quite different from unmarried love.

Not surprisingly, the wedding of Will and Willma was conducted according to laws not of their making. For our purposes here, we need only note that those laws have a long history in western civilization, being rooted in the Roman Empire. Already in the sixth century, the Emperor Justinian decreed that the only thing that was required for a valid marriage was the mutual consent of both parties.[13] In Roman law, a marriage is created by mutual consent, not by sexual intercourse, as it was in many of the northern European tribes. That difference of opinion as to what constitutes a marriage eventually created a widespread legal discussion in Europe, the conclusion of which has major impact on the marriage of Will and Willma. That question, which could easily be answered by the two lovers, is the *canonico-legal* question of when precisely their marriage is valid so that it is also indissoluble.

We already know the ancient Roman answer to the question: mutual consent between the parties makes marriages. We know also the ancient Northern European answer: sexual intercourse between the spouses after the giving of consent makes a marriage. Both answers have long histories; both may be supported by good reasons. In twelfth-century Europe, there were brilliant proponents of both points of view. Then, in mid-century, Gratian, the Master of the University of Bologna, proposed a compromise solution which combined both views. Consent initiates a marriage; subsequent sexual intercourse completes or consummates it. This compromise opinion settled the debate and is today still enshrined in the *Code of Canon Law* that governs marriages in the Roman Catholic Church (Can 1061). We shall have occasion to ponder the implications of this law in a later chapter. For the moment, we note only this single implication: when Will and Willma have given their consent one to the other, and when the wedding ceremony is over, they are not nearly as indissolubly married as they or most everyone else thinks.

Consent initiates marriage and consummation completes it. But what *is* the marriage into which Will and Willma have entered? Two definitions, again Roman in origin, have dominated the western discussion of this question. The first is found in Justinian's *Digesta* (23,2,1) and is attributed to the third-century jurist, Modestinus: "Marriage is a union of a man and a woman, and a communion of the whole of life, a participation in divine and human law." The second is found in the same emperor's *Instituta* (1,9,1), and is attributed to Modestinus' contemporary, Ulpianus: "Marriage is a union of a man and a woman, embracing an undivided communion of life."

Though the two "definitions" are really only generic descriptions of a long-existing social institution in Roman culture, they subsequently controlled discussions about marriage in western culture. They agree on the bedrock: marriage is a union (*coniunctio*) and, though the words are different in each definition, a union and a communion embracing the whole of life. That phrase, "the whole of life," is ambiguous, open to two different, if not unconnected, interpretations, and has been interpreted in two ways. It can mean as long as life lasts, and then implies that marriage is a lifelong commitment. It can mean everything that the spouses have, and then implies that nothing is left unshared between them. Over the years, both meanings have been interwoven, so that marriage is looked upon as the union of a man and a woman embracing the sharing of all goods until death, whether material or spiritual. In the freshness of their love, Will and Willma certainly approach it in that way. Their mutual well-wishing love impels them to promise marital communion in everything "until death do us part."

In modern times it has become fashionable to be cynical about the marital promise "until death do us part," not only because divorce statistics make a mockery of it but also because, so it is argued, unconditional promises covering a period of forty or fifty years just are not possible. To promise I will do something next week is one thing; to promise I will do it fifty years from now, when so much will have changed, is quite an impossible other. Only conditional promises, only those marital promises that are made on the condition that there be no change in either spouse, so the argument runs, can be made with any moral weight. I disagree.

The claim that the marriage vow "until death do us part" is somehow impossible is false. It is perfectly possible for Will and Willma to commit themselves unconditionally, for commitment is a statement of present intention, not an act of future clairvoyance. Love, as we have seen, is not an airy sentiment, but an act of the will, wishing well to another self. It is not true that either Will or Willma, especially if they are appropriately named Will and Willma, is helpless when and if one or the other wavers in marital commitment, even if one or the other or both have moved beyond their present standpoint. It is entirely possible that principles, freely chosen and willingly embraced now, can continue to be freely chosen and willingly embraced fifty years hence in substantially changed circumstances. History is full of examples. I cite three.

I offer as a first, widespread example prisoners of conscience. Contemporary history has made heroes of many of them: Dietrich Bonhoeffer, Nelson Mandela, Andre Sacharov. For our purposes here, however, we choose a literary hero, Addison's Cato. When offered life, freedom and the friendship of Caesar, and asked to name his terms, he replied thus: "Bid him disband his legions, restore the commonwealth to liberty . . . and stand the judgment of a Roman Senate. Bid him do this and Cato is his friend."[14] Like any other human, Cato valued life, liberty and friendship. He valued, however, not just *any* life. He had opted for the life of honor and, from that moment of freely chosen and freely embraced commitment, life without honor was no longer a real option for him. The principles of the life he had chosen, and to which he willed to be faithful, did not permit it.

The second, equally widespread example is soldiers going off to war. Like Cato, and us too, the soldier values life and liberty and easy living, but like Cato he does not value them at any cost. He also has committed himself to the principle of honor, and at any cost he will be faithful to that principle. He even enunciates his principle to his distraught lover as he marches off to war. "I could not love thee, dear, so much, loved I not honor more."[15] That same declaration has been made for centuries by a third group, married women and men who have freely chosen and freely embraced love and honor and who have willed to be faithful to these values "for better, for worse, for richer, for poorer, in sickness and in health, until death do us part." Our exemplary young man and young woman, appropriately named Will and Willma in celebration of a matter of will and not of sentiment, properly embrace these same principles on their wedding day. If they are to be faithful to those principles, they must listen to the advice we gave earlier in this chapter.

Love and marriage are a lot like a flower garden. It is never enough to plant the seeds and then to sit back and wait for the flowers to grow. The seeds must be lovingly watered and fed, the garden must be assiduously weeded if a beautiful garden is to grow. So it is with love and marriage. If they are to grow into a thing of beauty, they must be watered and nurtured and weeded by lovers and spouses. Friends and lovers must work unceasingly at friendship and love, they must care for them, nurture them jealously and sustain them, for they will not sustain themselves. Will and Willma must work unceasingly to nurture and sustain their marriage, for old, unnurtured marriages are a lot like old soldiers: they simply fade away, promise and love and honor notwithstanding.

One final consideration completes this section. We must ask not only what marriage *is* but what is it *for*? As we shall deal with that question in some detail in our final chapter, we shall answer here only summarily. In both the western and the Catholic traditions, marriage is held to have two purposes or ends. These ends are consistently articulated, from Augustine to the twentieth century, as they are in the 1917 *Code of Canon Law*. "The primary end of marriage is the procreation and nurture of children; its secondary end is mutual help and the remedying of concupiscence" (Can 1013,1).

The *Code* did not invent this hierarchy of ends;[16] it merely repeated it from a long history. This explicit hierarchy of ends, implicitly establishing also a subordination of ends, gave rise to a moral principle. Where a conflict arises between the fulfillment of the primary end of procreation and the secondary end of marital love and support, the secondary end must always give way to the primary. Will and Willma should be aware that, in the twentieth century, it has become a common experience that sustaining the primary end is frequently in conflict with and destructive of the secondary end, and sometimes of the marriage itself. They should know also that, at least in the Catholic Church, the second half of our century has brought a significant change.

The Second Vatican Council met each fall from 1962 to 1965 to consider the teachings of the Catholic Church. Among the many questions raised and answered was the one that concerns us presently, namely, the ends of marriage. In its *Pastoral Constitution on the Church in the Modern World,* the Council taught that both the institution of marriage and the marital love of the spouses "are ordained for the procreation and education of children, and find in them their ultimate crown" (GS 48). Given western intellectual history, there is nothing surprising there. There is something surprising, however, in the Council's approach to the primary-secondary ends terminology.

Despite insistent demands to reaffirm the traditional, hierarchical terminology, the Council refused to do so. Indeed, the Commission that prepared the final formulation of the Pastoral Constitution was careful to explain explicitly that the text cited above was not to be read as suggesting a hierarchy of ends in any way.[17] The Council itself taught explicitly that procreation "does not make the other ends of marriage of less account" and that marriage "is not instituted solely for procreation" (GS 50). The intense debates that took place in the Preparatory Commission and in the executive sessions of the Council itself make it impossible to claim that the refusal to speak of a hierarchy of ends in marriage was the result of some lapse of memory. There is not the slightest doubt that it was the result of deliberate choice.

Any possible doubt was definitively removed in 1983 with the publication of the revised *Code of Canon Law*. The *Church in the Modern World* had described marriage, in language whose parentage in Justinian, is obvious in this way: it is an "intimate partnership of married life and love

. . . established by the Creator and qualified by his laws. It is rooted in the conjugal covenant of irrevocable personal consent. Hence, by that human act whereby spouses mutually bestow and accept each other, a relationship arises which by divine will and in the eyes of society too is a lasting one'' (GS 48). The *Code* picked up this description and repeated it, declaring that ''the marriage covenant, by which a man and a woman establish between themselves a partnership of their whole life, and which of its very nature is ordered to the well-being of the spouses and to the procreation and upbringing of children, has, between the baptized, been raised by Christ the Lord to the dignity of a sacrament'' (Can 1055,1). These two documents sum up for now the essence of marriage. It is a partnership of love for the whole of life, ordered equally to the well-being of the spouses and to the generation and nurture of children. The discovery of this essence concludes this section and leads us into the next, for when such a marriage is between two believing Christians, the Catholic Church teaches, it is also a sacrament.

The Sacrament of Marriage

In the Bible there is an action called a prophetic symbol. Jeremiah, for instance, buys a potter's earthen flask, dashes it to the ground before a startled crowd, and proclaims the meaning of his action. ''Thus says the Lord of hosts: so will I break this people and this city, as one breaks a potter's vessel'' (Jer 19:11). Ezekiel takes a brick, draws a city on it, builds siegeworks around the city and lays siege to it. This city, he explains, is ''even Jerusalem'' (Jer 4:1) and his action ''a sign for the house of Israel'' (Jer 4:3). He takes a sword, shaves his hair with it and divides the hair into three bundles. One bundle he burns, another he scatters to the wind, a third he carries around Jerusalem shredding into even smaller pieces, explaining his action in the proclamation: ''This is Jerusalem'' (Jer 5:5).

The prophetic explanations clarify for us the meaning of the prophetic symbol. It is a human action which proclaims, makes explicit and celebrates in representation the action of God. Jeremiah's shattering of the pot is God's shattering of Jerusalem. Ezekiel's action is not the besieging of a brick but, again, God's overthrowing of Jerusalem. The prophetic symbol is a representative action, an action which proclaims and reveals in representation another, more crucial action. It is a representative symbol.

Prophetic, symbolic action is not limited to those few named prophets. Israel, a prophetic people, performed prophetic, symbolic actions. In the solemn *seder* meal, for instance, which was established as the memorial of the Exodus (Exod 12:14), the head of the gathered family takes unleavened bread and explains, "This is the bread of affliction our fathers ate in Egypt." It was at such a meal, the New Testament reports, that Jesus took bread and, when he had prayed in thanksgiving, broke it and proclaimed "This is my body which is for you. Do this in remembrance of me" (1 Cor 11:23-24). It is difficult not to notice the semantic correspondence between "this is Jerusalem," "this is the bread of affliction," and "this is my body." It is difficult to avoid the conclusion that each action is equally a prophetic, symbolic action.

Self-understanding in Israel was rooted in the great covenant between the god Yahweh and the people Israel. It is easy to predict that Israelites, prone to prophetic action, would search for such an action to symbolize their covenant relationship with Yahweh. It is just as easy, perhaps, to predict that the symbol they would choose is the covenant that is marriage between a man and a woman. The prophet Hosea was the first to speak of marriage as prophetic symbol of the covenant.

On a superficial level, the marriage of Hosea and his wife Gomer is like many marriages. But on a level beyond the superficial, Hosea interpreted it as a prophetic symbol, proclaiming, making humanly explicit and celebrating in representation the covenant communion between Yahweh and Israel. As Gomer left Hosea for other lovers, so too did Israel leave Yahweh for other gods. As Hosea waits in faithfulness for Gomer's return, as he receives her back without recrimination, so too does Yahweh wait for and take back Israel. Hosea's human action and reaction is prophetic symbol of Yahweh's divine action and reaction. In both covenants, the human and the divine, the covenant relationship has been violated, and Hosea's actions both mirror and reflect Yahweh's. In symbolic representation, they proclaim, reveal and celebrate not only Hosea's faithfulness to Gomer but also Yahweh's faithfulness to Israel.

Contemporary feminist theologians rightly object to the allegorization of the story of the marriage of Hosea and Gomer which establishes Hosea, and all husbands, in the place of the faithful God, and Gomer, and all wives, in the place of faithless Israel. The story is not such a linear allegory, but a variegated parable whose meanings remain always to be discovered anew in each changing circumstance. One constant meaning is clear if mysterious, not so much for Gomer and Hosea as for their marriage. Not only is it a universal human institution; it is also a religious, prophetic symbol, proclaiming, revealing and celebrating in the human world the communion between God and God's people. Not only is it law, it is also grace and redemption. Lived within this context of grace, lived within faith as we might say today, marriage appears as a two-tiered reality. On one tier, it signifies the mutually covenanted love of this man and this woman, of Hosea and Gomer, of Will and Willma; on another it prophetically symbolizes the mutually covenanted love of God and God's people. This two-tiered view of marriage became the Christian view, found for instance in the Letter to the Ephesians, which we shall analyze in detail in Chapter Three. Jewish prophetic symbol became in history Christian sacrament.

The classical Roman Catholic definition of sacrament, "an outward sign of inward grace instituted by Christ," which took a thousand years to become established,[18] can now be more fully explicated. A sacrament is a prophetic symbol in and through which the Church, the Body of Christ, proclaims, reveals and celebrates in representation that presence and action of God which is called grace. To say that a marriage between Christians is a sacrament is to say, then, that it is a prophetic symbol, a two-tiered reality. On one level, it proclaims, reveals and celebrates the intimate communion of life and love between a man and a woman, between our Will and Willma. On another, more profound level, it proclaims, makes explicit and celebrates the intimate communion of life and love and grace between God and God's people and between Christ and Christ's people, the Church.

A couple entering any marriage say to one another, before the society in which they live, "I love you and I give myself to and for you." A Christian couple entering a specifically sacramental marriage say that, too, but they also say more. They say, "I love you as Christ loves his church, steadfastly and faithfully." From the first, therefore, a Christian marriage is intentionally more than just the communion for the whole of life of this man and this woman. It is more than just human covenant; it is also religious covenant. It is more than law and obligations and rights; it is also grace. From the first, God and God's Christ are present as third partners in it, modeling it, gracing it and guaranteeing it. This presence of grace in its most ancient and solemn Christian sense, namely, the presence of the gracious God, is not something extrinsic to Christian marriage. It is something essential to it, something without which it would not be *Christian* marriage at all. Christian, sacramental marriage certainly proclaims the love of Will and Willma. It also proclaims, reveals and celebrates their love for their God and for the Christ they confess as Lord. It is in this sense that it is a sacrament, a prophetic symbol, both a sign and an instrument, of the explicit and gracious presence of Christ and of the God he reveals.

In every symbol there are, to repeat, two levels of meaning. There is a foundational level and, built on this foundation, a symbolic level. The foundational level in a sacramental marriage is the loving communion for the whole of life between a man and a woman who are disciples of Christ and members of his Church. The symbolic or sacramental level is the representation in their communion of the communion of life and love between Christ and his Church. This two-tiered and connected meaningfulness is what is meant by the claim that marriage between Christians is a sacrament. In a truly Christian marriage, which is to be understood as a marriage between two *believing* Christians, the symbolic meaning takes precedence over the foundational meaning, in the sense that the steadfast love of God and of Christ is actively present as the model for the love of the spouses. In and through their love, God and God's Christ are present in a Christian marriage, gracing the spouses with their presence and providing for them models of steadfast and abiding love. I shall examine this love in a later chapter.

There is one, final question for this chapter. When the Catholic Church claims that *marriage* between baptized Christians is a sacrament, what precisely is the meaning of the word *marriage*? In ordinary language, the word is ambiguous. Sometimes it refers to the wedding ceremony, in which Will and Willma freely commit to one another "for the purpose of establishing a marriage" (Can 1057,2). Sometimes it means, more crucially, the marriage and the life that flows from their wedding commitment, the communion of life and love that lasts until death. Both these common meanings of the word *marriage* are intended in the claim that marriage is a sacrament. The everyday meanings of this claim will be considered in the next chapter.

Summary

This chapter was about four interrelated personal realities: friendship, love, marriage and the sacrament of marriage. It supported Aristotle's ancient claim that human life is impossible without friends, trusted others who understand and accept me as I am, who challenge my potential and who rejoice with me when I attain it and console me when I don't. Such friends wish me well, that is they love me, and I love them. We share our thoughts, our feelings, our dreams and, on occasion, because we wish, like Will and Willma, to be best friends for life, we marry. The chapter argued that marriage is an intimate partnership of love for the whole of life, equally ordered to the mutual well-being of the spouses and to the generation and nurture of children. It argued further that when marriage is between believing Christians, it is also a sacrament, that is, a prophetic symbol of the presence of the graceful and gracious God in the world. Every marriage between Christian believers offers, therefore, two levels of meaning. There is a first, foundational level, the communion of the whole of life between the spouses; and, built upon this foundation there is a second, symbolic level, on which the communion between the spouses images and represents the communion between Christ and his Church. It is about this sacrament of marriage that this book is concerned.

Questions for Reflection

1. How do you personally define friendship and friends? Does your definition alter in any way the discussion in this chapter?

2. How do you define love? Does your definition agree in any way with the claim that love is a matter of the will, reaching out to the good in others and wishing them well?

3. How do you understand the definition of marriage as "the union of a man and a woman, and a communion of the whole of life"? Is such a definition, in your opinion, still valid in our world?

4. In general, what do you understand to be the meaning of the word *sacrament*? In particular, what do you understand to be the meaning of the Catholic teaching that the marriage between two Christian believers is a sacrament of the union between Christ and his Church?

5. How do you understand the relationship between the marriage of Will and Willma and the sacrament of marriage which they would celebrate? What are the differences, if any, between the two?

NOTES

1. *The Nicomachean Ethics,* 8, 1.

2. Ibid., 8, 3.

3. Ibid. Cf. Aquinas *In III Sent.,* d.27,q.2,a.1,ad 8: "amicitia est redamantium" (friendship is between those who love mutually).

4. B. Jowett, *The Dialogues of Plato* (New York: Random House, 1937) 1:51-52.

5. Lilian B. Rubin, *Just Friends: The Role of Friendship in Our Lives* (New York: Harper and Row, 1985) 7.

6. Erik H. Erikson, *Childhood and Society* (New York: Norton, 1963) 247-274.

7. ST I,20,1 ad 3.

8. ST, Ia–IIae,q.26,a.4,corp.

9. ST,Ia,19,3 ad 6. In his "Le desir du bonheur et l'existence de Dieu," *Revue des Sciences Philosophiques et Theologiques* 13 (1924) 163, M. Roland-Gosselin cites fifty similar citations spanning Aquinas' entire career.

10. *De Amicitia* 6,22: "quid dulcius, quam habere, quicum omnia audias sic loqui, ut tecum?"; and 7,23: "verum etiam amicum qui intuetur, tamquam exemplar aliquod intuetur sui."

11. *Nicomachean Ethics* 8,2; ST,II–II,23,1 corp.

12. Robert O. Johann, *The Meaning of Love* (Westminster: Newman Press, 1955) 36.

13. *Justiniani Digesta* 35,1,15.

14. Cited in J. Casey, "Actions and Consequences," *Morality and Moral Reasoning* (London: Methuen, 1971) 201.

15. Richard Lovelace, "Song to Lucasta. Going to the Wars," *Seventeenth Century Prose and Poetry*, ed. Robert P. Coffin (New York: Harcourt Brace, 1946) 193.

16. See, however, Urban Navarrette, "Structura Juridica Matrimonii Secundum Concilium Vaticanum II," *Periodica* 56 (1967) 366. Navarette argues that the *Code of Canon Law* is the first official document of the Roman Catholic Church to so order hierarchically the ends of marriage. Whether that claim is true or not, it is clearly not the first hierarchical ordering of the ends in western theological and legal history.

17. See Bernhard Haring, *Commentary on the Documents of Vatican II* (New York: Herder, 1969) 5:234.

18. See Michael G. Lawler, *Symbol and Sacrament: A Contemporary Sacramental Theology* (New York: Paulist, 1987) 29–34.

2

The Sacrament of Marriage: Meanings

The Matrix of the Sacrament of Marriage

The first chapter dealt with the marriage of Will and Willma and the sacramentality embedded in it. This second chapter inquires more fully into the meanings inherent in that sacramentality. I do two things in this opening section. First, I ask what is the human matrix of the sacrament of marriage, what is "the human conduct, conduct perhaps formed into a ritual, that is taken and made into the sacrament"?[1] Secondly, I respond to this question by concluding that the matrix is the mutual love of Will and Willma. It is from that matrix, informed by Christian faith, as we shall see in the next section, that the sacrament of marriage takes its religious meanings.

Consideration of the human matrix of the sacrament of marriage arises naturally out of the traditional Catholic doctrine that every saving event is two-dimensional. The salvation of women and men is always a grace, a gift from the God who is confessed as Father, Son and Holy Spirit; it is also a gift which women and men must themselves realize in free cooperation (DS 370–397). Every saving event has these two dimensions: the self-gift of God through Christ in the Spirit (that is, grace), and the free acceptance of this gift by believers coupled with their self-gift in return through Christ in the Spirit to God. The saving event that is a sacrament is no exception, including the sacrament that is Christian marriage. A sacrament is not a thing which believers receive. It is, rather, a graced interaction in and through which they express both their acceptance of the gracious gift of God and their gift of themselves to God in return. The sacramental marriage of Will and Willma is such an outward sign of the gift or grace of God and the gift of selves in return.

Though it did not deal in any detail with the meaning of the sacrament of marriage, the Second Vatican Council did provide material to illumine the matrix of such marriage. Marriage, it taught, is "a community of love . . . an intimate partnership of marital life and love" (GS 47–48). Marriage, as we saw in the previous chapter, is essentially a community of love. The mutual love of the spouses, and their passionate desire to be best friends forever, is of the very essence of marriage. It is, therefore, equally of the essence of the sacrament of marriage.

If marriage is rooted ultimately in the mutual love of the spouses, it is rooted proximately, as we also saw in the previous chapter, in the "irrevocable personal consent" (GS 48), which ritually expresses that love. When faced with demands to describe that consent as legal *contract*, the Vatican Council demurred and chose to describe it rather as personal *covenant*. This choice situates both marriage and the sacrament of marriage as personal, rather than as juridical, realities, and adorns them with nuances of the biblical covenants between God and Israel and Christ and the Church. The interpersonal character of the marriage covenant is further underscored by the formal object of the covenant. The Council declares that the spouses "mutually bestow and accept each other" (GS 48), rejecting the legal formulation of the 1917 Code of Canon Law that each "gives and accepts a perpetual and exclusive right over the body for acts which are themselves suitable for the generation of children" (Can 1081,2). The revised Code of Canon Law replicates the Council's teaching that the spouses mutually give and accept each other, adding that such gifts are "for the purpose of establishing a marriage" (Can 1057,2).

If the 1917 *Code of Canon Law* is considered carefully, one could be forgiven for assuming that a man and a woman who hated one another could be married, as long as each gave to the other the right over her or his body. In December 1930, in his influential encyclical on Christian marriage *Casti Connubii*, Pope Pius XI scorned such nonsense by underscoring the place of love in marriage. This love, he taught, does not consist "in pleasing words only, but in the deep attachment of the heart which is expressed in action, since love is proved by deeds."[2] Will and Willma, together with every other lover, will have no difficulty understanding this teaching.

The Fathers of the Second Vatican Council devote an entire section to the love which founds marriage and sacrament. They begin by drawing on the common tradition of the Old and New Testaments, in which love is central. They interpret the *Song of Songs* as a canticle to human, including sexual, love, rather than to divine, mystical love, the reading which had long been modestly traditional in both Jewish and Christian hermeneutic. This marital love is "eminently human," involves "the good of the whole person,'' and is ''steadfastly true.'' It is singularly expressed and perfected in sexual intercourse, which signifies and promotes ''that mutual self-giving by which the spouses enrich one another'' (GS 49). It is not idly that we say in everyday language that the mutual self-giving of the spouses in sexual intercourse is ''making love.''

In 1970, the Roman Rota, the supreme marriage tribunal of the Catholic Church, removed all doubt about the centrality of mutual love in constituting both marriage and the sacrament of marriage. They ruled that ''where marital love was lacking, either the consent is not free, or it is not internal, or it excludes or limits the object which must be integral to have a valid marriage.'' They concluded that ''lack of marital love is the same as lack of consent. Marital love has juridical force here, because the defendant despised the total communion of life which primarily and of itself constitutes the object of the marriage contract'' (or covenant).[3]

In our day, both marriage and the sacrament of marriage are situated in a matrix which Will and Willma, and every other married person, can recognize. In cooperation with the gift of God, spouses co-create their marriages by consenting to one another as best friends in a covenant for the whole of life, in which they give and accept gifts of love as warrants of their gifts of self. It is this mutual, covenantal and marital love, ritually expressed in the exchange of consent in the wedding ceremony and in a thousand acts of loving conduct throughout their lives, that provides the human matrix which is taken up and transformed into sacrament.

There is danger of anachronism here, which can lead to the mistaking of the word *love*. In contemporary usage, love means a strong affection for another self, frequently a passionate affection for a person of the opposite sex. We have earlier described it as wishing well to another with whom we passionately desire to be best friends. In the Bible that well-wishing is specified as ''loyalty, service and obedience.''[4] We merely note this here as a warning against anachronism; we shall explain it in detail in the biblical analysis of the next chapter. We proceed now to an explication of the notion of covenant, in which the mutual love of Will and Willma is expressed and in which their marriage and sacrament is constituted.

The Covenant of Marriage

To covenant is to consent and to commit oneself radically and solemnly. When Will and Willma covenant in the sacrament of marriage, they commit themselves mutually to a life of equal and intimate partnership in loyal and faithful love. They commit themselves mutually to create and to sustain a climate of personal openness, availability and trust. They commit themselves mutually to rules of behavior which will respect, nurture and sustain intimate communion and steadfast love. They commit themselves mutually to explore together the religious depth of human life in general, and of their marriage in particular, and to respond to that depth in the light of their shared Christian faith. They commit themselves mutually to abide in love, in covenant, in marriage and in sacrament for the whole of life.[5]

In sacramental marriage, Will and Willma commit themselves to create a life of equal and intimate partnership in loyal and faithful love. When God created the heavens and the earth, when no plant had yet sprung up from the earth because God had not yet brought rain, a mist rose up and watered the earth. The mist turned the dry earth to mud, in Hebrew *'adamah*, and from that *'adamah* God formed *'adam* and breathed into *'adam's* nostrils the breath of life. And *'adam* became a living being (Gen 2:4-7). "When the Lord Yahweh created *'adam*, he made *'adam* in the likeness of Yahweh. Male and female he created them, and he blessed them and he named them *'adam*" (Gen 5:1-2).

This myth, for it is indeed a myth and not historical description, responds to the perennial human question: where did we come from? We, in Hebrew *'adam*, in English *humankind*, came from God. Male and female as we are, we are from God, and together we make up humankind. This fact alone, that God names woman and man together *'adam*, establishes the equality of men and women as human beings.

The other *Genesis* myth which speaks of the creation of woman from man's rib, intends in the Hebrew metaphor to emphasize the equality of man and woman, not their separate creation. The Catholic bishops of the United States underscore this fact in their pastoral response to the concerns of women in the Church. Since "in the divine image . . . male and female (God) created them" (Gen 1:27), woman and man are equal in human dignity and favor in God's eyes. They are equal in everything that is human; they are "bone of bone and flesh of flesh" (Gen 2:23). It is only because they are so equal, says the myth, that they may marry and "become one body" (Gen 2:24).

As western Christians have seriously misread the Hebrew myth about equal man and woman, so too have they seriously misread the Hebrew notion of body. They have linked it much too exclusively to one facet of becoming one in marriage, namely, the joining of bodies in sexual union. This facet is an important part of becoming one, uniting bodies to express and create the union of persons, but it is far from all there is.

In the Hebrew myth, *body* does not refer to the external, physical part of the human being, as it does in English. It refers instead to the whole person. In marriage, therefore, a man and a woman covenant to unite not only their bodies but also their persons. Marriage is for the good of persons, not for the good of bodies. In the Hebrew culture of Jesus' time, in distinction to contemporary western culture where individuals consent to a marriage which society guarantees as a legal reality, families consented to a marriage which society guaranteed as a blood relationship. That blood relationship makes the spouses one body, one person, in a way that escapes the understanding of those who think only in physical and legal terms. They become, as God intended in the beginning, equal man and woman complementing one another to recreate together *'adam* and the image of God. Rabbis have long taught that, according to God's design, neither man nor woman is wholly human until each receives the complement of the other in marriage. The equal partnership of marriage is demanded by the founding myth in which both Judaism and Christianity are rooted.

Christian marital covenant demands not only the creation of a life of equal partnership but also the sustaining of that life. As the God of Jesus is not a deist God who creates and then abandons creation to its own laws, as Jesus is not a Christ who gives himself up for the Church (Eph 5:25) and then abandons her, so no Christian believer creates a marriage and leaves it to survive by itself. When Will and Willma marry, they commit themselves mutually to create rules of behavior which will nurture and sustain their marriage. As believing Christians, they will come to those rules by paying careful attention to their tradition.

There is a sound and correct effort across the Christian traditions to move away from what may be called a "biblical rules" approach to morality. "Realizing the impossibility of transposing rules from biblical times to our own, interpreters look for larger themes, values or ideals which can inform moral reflection without determining specific practices in advance."[6] Will and Willma, and all who are married, will find the ideals to inform their covenant marriage succinctly summarized in the biblical Letter to the Ephesians. The author critiques the list of traditional household duties in first century Palestine, together with the inequality embedded in it, and challenges all Christians to "give way to one another because you stand in awe of Christ" (5:21). The critique both challenges the absolute authority of any Christian individual over another, including that of a husband over a wife, and establishes the basic attitude required of all Christians, even if they be husband and wife, namely, an awe of Christ and a giving way to one another because of it.

Since all Christians are to give way to one another, it is not surprising that wives are challenged to give way to their husbands (5:22). What is surprising, at least to husbands who see themselves as lords and masters of their wives and who seek to found this unchristian attitude, is the challenge to husbands in Ephesians. The challenge is that "the husband is the head of the wife *as* (that is, in the same way as) Christ is head of the church" (5:23). In immediate response to the obvious question, "how is Christ head of the church?," the writer explains, "he gave himself up for her" (5:25). There is here a clear echo of a self-description Jesus offers in Mark's gospel: "the Son of Man came not to be served but to serve" (10:45). There is a loud echo also of what Jesus constantly pointed out to his power-hungry disciples, namely, that in the kingdom of God the leader is the servant of all (Luke 22:26).

The Christian way to exercise authority is to serve. Christ-like authority is not absolute control over another human being; it is not making unilateral decisions and transmitting them to another to carry out; it is not reducing another to the status of a slave. To be head as Christ is head is to serve. The Christian husband, as Markus Barth puts it so beautifully, is called to be "the first servant of his wife,"[7] and she is equally called to be his first servant. One rule of behavior by which Will and Willma may nurture both their marriage and their sacrament is the Christian rule of service, of God, of one another, and of the needs around them.

Another Christian rule for behavior, both in and out of marriage, is the great commandment: "You shall love your neighbor as yourself" (Lev 19:18; Mark 12:31). Husbands, the Letter to the Ephesians instructs, are to "love their wives as their own bodies," for the husband "who loves his wife loves himself" (5:28). We can rightfully assume that the same instruction is intended also for wives. The great Torah and Gospel commandment to love one's neighbor as oneself applies in marriage to one's spouse who, in that most beautiful and most sexual of Jewish love songs, the *Song of Songs*, is addressed nine times as *plesion*—"neighbor" (1:9,15;2:2,10,13;4:1,7;5:2;6:4). "Neighbor," in the *Song*, is a term of endearment for the beloved. A paraphrase of Paul clinches the rule of love for Christian spouses: those who love their spouses have fulfilled all the rules of behavior for nurturing and sustaining a Christian marriage (Rom 13:8). I shall specify this love in the next chapter.

A sacramental marriage is not just a wedding to be celebrated. It is also, and more critically, an equal and loving partnership to be lived for the whole of life. When Will and Willma covenant to one another in the sacrament of marriage, they commit themselves to explore together the religious depth of their married life and to respond to that depth in the light of their mutual covenant to Christ and to the Church in which he abides.

One of the central affirmations of Christian faith is the affirmation of discipleship. "Disciple" is a gospel word, always implying both a call from Jesus and a response from a believer. Disciples are dedicated to be learners, and the disciples of Jesus are learners of a triple mystery. They ponder the mystery of the Spirit-God who calls them to know and to love and to serve, the mystery of the Christ in whom this God is embodied and revealed, the mystery of the Church, which is the Body of Christ (Eph 1:22-23; Col 1:18,24), and which calls them to communion and to service. Will and Willma, members of the Church, disciples of the Christ and believers in the God he reveals, consent in covenant to ponder together these mysteries and to discover their implications for life.

Marriage does not isolate the spouses from life. It immerses them in life, and confronts them with the ultimate questions of life and death that are the stuff of religion. Sometimes the questions are easy, concerning things like happiness, friends, success, the birth of children; sometimes they are difficult, concerning pain, suffering and alienation, fear, grief and death. Always life demands that sense be made of the questions; marriage demands that the spouses make sense of them together; Christian marriage demands that they make sense of them in the light of their shared Christian faith.

As Will and Willma find adequate Christian responses to the questions that life and marriage impose upon them, they mutually nurture one another in Christian discipleship. They learn and grow together in Christian maturity. The more they mature the more they come to grasp the ongoing nature of their marriage as sacrament. They come to realise that, though their marriage is already *a* sacramental sign of the covenant between Christ and his Church, it is not yet the *best* sign it can be. That best sign takes time. In Christian marriage, even more than in any other marriage, the answer to the age old question of when are two people married is simple: a lifetime after they exchange consent.

As disciples in our age, Will and Willma have to learn and decide what sign their marriage will offer to a world that is sinful, broken and divided by racism, sexism and classism. Since they are believing Christians, that sign will depend, at least in part, on Jesus' assertion, already considered, that he came "not to be served but to serve" (Mark 10:45). No Christian, individual, couple or church, can be anything less than servants for others. No Christian family can be anything less than a "domestic church" (LG 11) for others, reaching out to heal the brokenness in the communities in which it exists. Service to the society in which they live is the responsibility of all Christians, married or unmarried. Sacramental marriage adds only the specification that the spouses exercise their service as part of their marital life.

We conclude this section, as we began it, with a characterization of marriage, only now a more fully elaborated characterization of *Christian* marriage. Christian marriage is an intimate and equal partnership of life and love. Its origin is, ultimately, in God's act of creating *'adam* male and female, proximately, in the covenant of the spouses' free consent; its goal is the continuation of Christ's mission to establish the reign of God in the lives of the spouses and their children, and in the world in which they live. Will and Willma are instructed about such marriage in the prayers of their wedding service. "Father, keep them always true to your commandments. Let them be living examples of Christian life. Give them the strength which comes from the gospels so that they may be witnesses of Christ to others."[8] If ritual prayers are always the best indicators of ritual meaning, and they are, there can be no doubt from this prayer about the meaning of Christian covenant and sacramental marriage.

Personal Faith and the Sacrament of Marriage

Nothing that is authentically Christian exists apart from Christian faith, not even sacrament, particularly not the adult sacrament of Christian marriage. Since that assertion will ring strangely in ears attuned to the notion of automatic sacramentality, it will need to be explained. There are four complementary theological facts commingled in the question of the relationship of personal faith and the sacrament of marriage. In this section I shall, first, enunciate the four as theses and, then, explicate each in turn. The four theses are: first, personal faith is required for salvation; second, the personal faith of the participant is required for the validity of any sacrament; third, the personal faith of the participants is required for the validity of the sacrament of marriage; fourth, the personal faith of the participants is required for right sacramental intention.

1. *Personal Faith and Salvation.* One cannot read the New Testament, even cursorily, without being impressed by its emphasis on the necessity of faith for salvation. The Gospels record that Jesus complained insistently about the absence of faith and just as insistently praised its presence (Matt 8:5-13; 8:23-27; 9:20-22; 17:19-21; 21:18-22; Mark 5:25-34; 6:1-6). Paul vehemently defended the necessity of personal faith for salvation (Rom 1:16-17; 3:26-30; 5:1; Gal 3:6-9). The tradition of the necessity of faith continued in the Church and flowered on both sides of the Reformation controversies.

Martin Luther made his stand on *sola fides*, faith alone. Though wishing to combat the Lutheran teaching that only faith and nothing more was necessary for salvation, the Council of Trent left no doubt about faith's necessity. "We may be said to be justified through faith, in the sense that 'faith is the beginning of human salvation,' the foundation and source of all justification, 'without which it is impossible to please God'

(Heb 11:6) and to be counted as his sons" (DS 1532). The same teaching is repeated in the important chapter on the sources of justification where baptism is described as "the sacrament of faith, without which no one has ever been justified" (DS 1529). The Latin text leaves no doubt that the phrase without which, *sine qua*, qualifies faith and not sacrament or baptism, both of which would require *sine quo*. There is no doubt that Trent wished to affirm the primacy of active, personal faith for salvation.

The firm Tridentine position notwithstanding, the polemical context of the times created a certain uneasiness in Roman Catholic assertions about the place of faith in the process of salvation and sanctification. Following Trent's lead of isolating and highlighting, in order to condemn, the error in the assertions of the Reformers, Counter-Reformation theologians advanced their theologies as overt counterpoint to those of the Reformation. Nowhere did this theological minimalism cause harm more than in sacramental theology, specifically in the matter of the need for personal faith to make a sacrament valid. That harm was most clearly evidenced in a very restricted understanding of the nature of the sacramental rite, the Scholastic *opus operatum*.[9]

2. *The Personal Faith of the Participant and Sacrament.* Trent defined two important ideas related to *opus operatum*. It taught, first, that "if anyone says that sacraments of the New Law do not contain the grace they signify or that they do not confer that grace on him who places no obstacle to it . . . let him be anathema" (DS 1606). It taught, secondly, that "if anyone says that grace is not conferred *ex opere operato* through the sacraments of the New Law, but that faith alone in the divine promises is sufficient to obtain grace: let him be anathema" (DS 1608).

In the years immediately preceding the convocations at Trent, nominalism was rampant in the theological disciplines. Nominalist theologians taught that the only thing a person receiving (sic) a sacrament need do was to place no obstacle to grace. This meant, in the popular thinking of the time, that all a person need do was be free from mortal sin; grace was then conferred by the correct enactment of the physical rite. It was just such a mechanical and reified understanding of sacrament that provided the basis for the objections of the Reformers about automatic grace, and led to their rejection of the very notion of *opus operatum*. Nominalist theologians, however, constituted a majority at Trent, and it was the nominalist definition that became "*the* exhaustive definition of the *opus operatum* of the efficacy of any sacrament."[10]

No real dichotomy between the rite and the contribution of the recipient to the rite, *opus operatum* and *opus operantis* respectively, can be found in the theological thinking of the great Scholastics. Aquinas frequently uses the concept *opus operatum* in his early *Commentary on the*

Sentences but never in the *Summa Theologiae*, his final work. This fact may be taken as indication that he did not consider the term necessary to the presentation of a mature sacramental theology. Indeed, "the truth that this terminology was intended to bring out was presented satisfactorily, and even in finer detail, in his Christological appreciation of the sacraments."[11]

The Christological character of a sacrament as an action of God in Christ is the fundamental doctrine underlying Thomas' understanding of sacrament. On this fundamental basis rest all other ways of using the phrase. Baptism, for instance, "justifies *ex opere operato*: this is not human's work but God's." Baptism has effect, not because of the merits of the person being baptized, "but because of the merits of Christ." It is efficacious "because of the passion of Christ."[12] It is not the external rite that effects grace, at least not as principal cause,[13] but the sacred reality that is signified by the external rite, namely, the gracious and saving action of God in Christ.

The technical notion, *opus operatum*, contrasts the constitution of a sacrament *qua* external sign in the Church and the subjective disposition of either the minister or the recipient. A sacrament is constituted as an external sign without any contribution on the part of either minister or recipient. It is not, however, constituted as an *efficacious* sign, that is, as a sign which actually mediates grace, without the personal contribution of the recipient. Since a sacrament is not just any sign of grace but specifically an efficacious sign, if it is not constituted as efficacious sign, then it is not constituted as valid sacrament.[14] For the great Scholastics, *opus operatum* and *opus operantis* were not dichotomized as they were to be later in the Counter-Reformation Church. They were essentially related. The latter was regarded as the "personal aspect in the justifying process of any sacrament, that aspect by which a free and responsible person accepted God's grace" offered in the efficacy of the former.[15]

A tradition in the Church, established as far back as the controversy between Augustine and Pelagius and verified regularly ever since, is that men and women are free persons and are graced, not against their will, but according to their free cooperation (DS 373–397). If they have no intention of personally receiving a sacrament, then no mere physical submission to a rite will constitute for them a saving sacrament. In such a case, though there is no doubt that a sacramental sign is objectively offered by God in Christ in the Church, there is equally no doubt that it is not rendered effective by the subject. The sacrament offered by God in the Church still signifies the saving action of God in Christ, but not as *concretely* significative, and therefore effective and sacramental, for *this* subject. The cooperating participation of the subject transforms the objective rite into an efficacious sign of the action of God in Christ, that is, it transforms it into valid sacrament.[16]

It is for the valid signification of a sacrament that the personal faith of the participant is required. The participant "must signify genuine acceptance of what the Church offers. Otherwise the sacrament is not a *concrete, practical* sign of the divine will to save all."[17] And since the Catholic tradition of the past millennium serenely accepts that sacraments cause by signifying, when they do not signify neither do they cause. And when they do not cause, they are not valid sacraments. It is not just, as Thomas and the Counter-Reformation theology would have it, that they are valid but fruitless sacraments. It is that they are fruitless precisely because they are not valid sacraments, that is, efficacious signs. The faith of the participant is required to make a sacrament fruitful because it is first of all required to make a sacrament a concrete and valid sign.[18]

A sacrament which is fully a sacrament is a sign, not only of the gracing action of God in Christ (*opus operatum*) but also of the free faith of the participant cooperating with grace in this ritual (*opus operantis*). A true sacrament requires the conjunction of both the one and the other, and only in such conjunction is there free, and therefore valid and fruitful, encounter between men and women and God. As Aquinas taught long ago: the passion of Christ, the saving activity of God, "achieves its effect in those to whom it is applied through faith and love and the sacraments of faith."[19]

3. *Personal Faith and the Sacrament of Marriage.* If what I argued in the preceding sections is correct, then the assertion of this section is already demonstrated. The active faith of the participants is an essential prerequisite not just for the fruitfulness of a sacrament but also for its very validity. That the Code of Canon Law's assertion—"a valid marriage contract cannot exist between baptized persons without its being by that very fact a sacrament" (Can 1055, 2)—is at odds with this theological assertion is of no great theological import. Law likes clarity and likes to create clarity even where there is none. Today, the faith-situation of the baptized is anything but clear, and the Church and its theologians recognize two kinds of baptized, believers and nonbelievers.[20] The two are easily distinguished theologically on the basis of the presence or absence of active personal faith. They ought never, therefore, to be as easily equated in law as they are in the Code.

Of course, in any given case the active faith or nonfaith of a baptized person, and the various shades in between, will not be easy to ascertain. But no amount of legal presumption will ever supply for lack of active faith and consequent lack of sacramentality.[21] Convinced of the necessity of faith for valid baptism, Augustine sought to make good the evident lack of infant faith in baptism by arguing that the faith of others, at root the faith of the whole Church, made good the infant's lack.[22] That argument cannot be applied in the case of marriage, for marriage is entirely different from infant baptism. In marriage, we are dealing with adults who are required to have an active faith to participate in any sacrament, baptism as well as marriage, as the scrutinies at the baptism of adults clearly demonstrate.

Human marriage is transformed into Christian sacrament, not merely by some legal effect of baptism, but also by the active faith of the marrying and married couple. Those who marry without active *Christian* faith, though baptized, marry also without *Christian* sacrament. A further elaboration and proof of the validity of that assertion follows from a brief consideration of the underlined adjective *Christian*. To be authentically true, that adjective requires explicit reference to Jesus, who is actively confessed as the Christ, and to the community of people called Church, which is actively confessed as Christ's Body in the world. God in Christ through the Spirit, Church in Christ through the Spirit: such is both the context and the content of grace which distinguishes the human institution of marriage from the sacrament of marriage.

In his magisterial *Jesus*, Schillebeeckx offers a clear statement of the place of the Christ within the scheme of things Christian. "The heart of Christianity is not just the abiding message of Jesus and its definitive relevance, but the persisting eschatological relevance of his person."[23] The person of Jesus the Christ, not just his memory or his message, is at the heart of everything that is Christian, including *Christian* sacrament, including the sacrament of *Christian* marriage.

In 1980 the Synod of Bishops considered the question of the relationship of faith and sacrament in marriage and gave quasi-unanimous support (201 *placet*, 3 *nonplacet*) to this proposition. "We have to take into account the engaged couple's degree of faith maturity and their awareness of doing what the Church does. This intention is required for sacramental validity. It is absent if there is not at least a minimal intention of believing with the Church." Sacramental marriage requires explicit reference to Christ, and therefore to God, and to Church. A sacrament is at its core a Christ-event.

The intention to participate in any sacrament is the intention to participate in a Christ-event. The intention to participate in the sacrament of Christian marriage is the intention to participate in, not merely a marriage, but specifically a marriage explicitly acknowledged as a Christ-event. To put it otherwise, in the words of Jean-Marie Tillard, "the request for a sacrament can never be the request for a purely external ritual that has no connection with the mystery of salvation. The request for a sacrament is a request for a 'rite that gives salvation.' "[24]

There is yet more to be said, for the request for a sacrament is the request not only for a Christ-event but also for a Christ-event in the Church. That Church is not only an institution which Christ founded, it is also a mystery, "a reality impregnated with the presence of God," as Pope Paul VI once beautifully put it.[25] That mystery embraces, among other theological claims, the claims that the Church is a communion of men and women who are incorporated into Christ and who share in his life; that it is a communion which embodies Christ in the present world; that it is a communion which is his very Body (cf. 1 Cor 6:12-20; 10:17; 12:12-27; Rom 12:4-5; Eph 1:22-23; 2:14-16; 3:6; 4:4-16; 5:22-30; Col 1:18-24; 2:19; 3:15). *Lumen Gentium Christus est*, proclaimed the Second Vatican Council in its Dogmatic Constitution on the Church. Christ is the light of nations, Christ is the sun, and the Church but a moon reflecting that sun's light (LG 1). All of this, Christ-sun and Church-moon, must be embraced in the intention to create not only a marriage but especially a Christian sacramental marriage. The human institution of marriage becomes the Christian sacrament of marriage "only if the future spouses freely consent to enter into married life by passing through Christ into whom they were incorporated in baptism."[26]

The key that opens the door to Christian sacramental meanings is not just the intention of the spouses to marry, but rather their intention informed by faith to be rooted in and to represent Christ and his Church. Consent may make marriage a secular institution, but it is Christian faith, a "comprehensive 'yes' to God's revealing himself as man's savior in Christ,"[27] that makes it also a sacrament.

L. Orsy states broadly the relationship of faith and sacramental validity. If the baptized person "has never accepted the Christian mysteries as real gifts from God, or never accepted God as revealing himself in human history, how can he responsibly and freely give and take the sacrament?"[28] If spouses have not personally accepted the mysteries of God in Christ in the Church, and their sacramental representation in Christian marriage, how can they ever accept marriage as a Christ-event, a salvation event, a "sign of the grace of God and the form of invisible grace?" Tillard states the relationship more precisely: "The request for a sacrament is always the request for a 'rite that gives salvation.' If it is not the request for a salvation rite, then it is not a request for a sacrament in the strict sense; and what the minister gives him in response to his request will not be 'sacramental' for him."[29]

It is not the naked intention to marry, even to marry in some religious rite, that makes valid Christian sacrament. It is the Christian faith-informed intention to marry in a ritual that publicly proclaims to the spouses, to the Church and to the world not only "I love you," but also "I love you in Christ and in his Church." That active and faith-informed proclamation creates not only a marriage but specifically a *Christian* marriage, and not only fruitful but also valid Christian marriage. The judgment of the International Theological Commission can stand as final conclusion to this section. "The personal faith of the contracting parties does not [by itself] constitute the sacramentality of matrimony, but the absence of personal faith compromises the validity of the sacrament."[30]

4. *Personal Faith and Right Sacramental Intention.* Great stress is laid in traditional sacramental theology on sacramental intention, the intention to do what the Church does in sacramental action. To intend to receive a sacrament, Will and Willma must intend what the Church intends by its sacrament. This short, but integral, section asks about the relationship between the intention traditionally required for the valid reception of sacrament and personal Christian faith. Put simply, the question is this: can one have a real intention to participate in a sacrament without, at least, minimal personal faith?

A pregnant phrase from the young Aquinas provides an answer: "faith directs intention, and without [faith] intention cannot be right."[31] Though intention and personal faith are not to be confused, they are not to be totally separated either. "The real intention," the International Theological Commission teaches, "is born from and feeds on living faith."[32] One cannot have a right sacramental intention without, at least, a minimal personal faith. Recalling the preceding section will substantiate this judgment. The right intention to participate in a sacrament is the intention to participate in a rite that gives salvation, a God-in-Christ and Christ-in-the-Church event. None of this, not God-in-Christ nor Christ-in-the-Church, can be intended without being, as least, minimally known and embraced in personal faith. The right intention to participate in a sacrament, therefore, requires a minimum of personal faith. When personal faith is absent, so too is right sacramental intention; and when right intention is absent, as the tradition universally holds, then there is no valid sacrament.

O'Callaghan underscores that "addressing the question of the sacramentality of the marriage of the nonbelieving baptized couple along the line of the absence of intention rather than that of the absence of faith keeps us within the parameters of what is a very firmly based theological tradition."[33] The theological judgment—no personal faith, no right intention—is a well-founded judgment. The conclusion that flows from it is equally well-founded theologically: without personal faith, there is no valid sacrament. Baptized nonbelievers cannot enter into a valid sacrament, not even the sacrament of marriage. As stated earlier, I am fully aware that this conclusion is at variance with the Code of Canon Law, which continues to cling to the juridical claim that "a valid marriage contract cannot exist between baptized persons without its being by that very fact a sacrament" (can. 1055, 2). Since I have demonstrated elsewhere the theological inaccuracy of this claim, I see no need to reprise that demonstration here.[34]

In reality, there is no theological debate about whether faith is necessary or not for sacramental validity. It is taken as a given that it is. The only debate is over what qualifies as faith. Many judge that faith cannot be reduced to "an explicit and conscious act of faith," and that a person "can posses the habit of faith . . . most especially through baptism."[35] This habit seals the new Christian's condition as "believer." That judgment rests on a classic Scholastic distinction which opens the word *fides*-faith to serious ambiguity and misunderstanding.

In the tradition derived from Scholasticism, faith refers either analogically to *virtus fidei*, the power of faith, or univocally to *actus fidei*, the explicit and conscious act of faith. A *virtus* is a habit,[36] a quality ordered to an act;[37] it is a power to act, a know-how to act. A virtue is a necessary prerequisite to a corresponding act, but it is not the act nor does the act ineluctably follow from the virtue. The Catholic tradition holds that it is the virtue or the know-how of faith that is bestowed in baptism.[38] For that virtue to become a personal act of faith, it must be activated, freely, explicitly, consciously and however minimally. It is a personal act of faith, always under the grace of God, that transforms the human being from one who has the power to be a believer into one who is actively a believer.

Baptism makes a person a "believer" only in the most derived and passive and analogical of sense. It bestows the virtue, the capacity, to become a believer. It is only an explicit and conscious personal act of faith, however, that makes anyone a believer in the primary sense of the word, namely, one who actually believes. It is in such active personal faith, and not just in the virtue of faith, that Will and Willma cooperate with God-in-Christ and Christ-in-the-church in the transformation of secular realities, including their marriage, into Christian sacraments. It is such active personal faith, again however minimal, that is required for right sacramental intention.

Summary

This chapter sought to illumine meanings inherent in the sacrament of marriage. It inquired as to the nature of the human substratum or matrix of the sacrament, and concluded that the matrix was the mutual love of the spouses leading to a partnership for the whole of life. It explicated that communion of love as a mutual covenant to a life of equal, intimate and loyal partnership. It sought, finally, to clarify the theological fact that marriage does not become sacrament without the cooperating personal faith of the spouses. From everything that has been said in this book so far, I would like Will and Willma to remember this: they can take for granted neither their foundational love and marriage nor the sacrament of marriage which their shared faith builds with God upon that foundation. Their mutual love of one another, their shared faith in the God revealed in Christ, and the sacrament raised upon both, need constantly to be nurtured; not only to grow and develop but even to survive.

Questions for Reflection

1. Every saving event has two dimensions: the self-gift of God through Christ in the Spirit (that is, grace) and the free acceptance of this gift by believers coupled with their self-gift in return through Christ in the Spirit to God. How is this fact relevant in the marriage of Will and Willma?

2. What implications do you see for Christian marriage in the judgment of the Roman Rota: "where marital love was lacking, either the consent is not free, or it is not internal, or it excludes or limits the object which must be integral to have a valid marriage"?

3. What do you understand now by the word "covenant"? What is the relationship between covenant and sacrament in the marriage of Will and Willma?

4. Christian faith is a person's comprehensive "yes" to God revealing himself as the person's savior in Christ. After the discussions in this chapter on the role of personal faith in creating a valid sacrament, what role do you see faith playing in the marriage of Will and Willma?

5. In your judgment, what difference does it make whether a marriage is lived simply as a social institution or as also a Christian sacrament?

NOTES

1. Theodore Mackin, *The Marital Sacrament: Marriage in the Catholic Church* (New York: Paulist, 1989) 11.

2. AAS 22 (1930) 348.

3. Cited from Paul F. Palmer, "Christian Marriage: Contract or Covenant?," *TS* 33 (1972) 647.

4. William Moran, "The Ancient Near Eastern Background of the Love of God in Deuteronomy," *Catholic Biblical Quarterly* 25 (1963) 82.

5. This section is inspired by Wilson Yates, "The Protestant View of Marriage," in *Journal of Ecumenical Studies* 22 (1985) 41–54.

6. Lisa S. Cahill, "Is Catholic Ethics Biblical?," Warren Lecture Series in Catholic Studies, No. 20 (University of Tulsa) 5–6.

7. *Ephesians.* The Anchor Bible (New York: Doubleday, 1974) 618.

8. *The Rites* (New York: Pueblo, 1976) 544.

9. It is significant that, when Leo XIII enthroned Scholasticism as the official way to do philosophy and theology, it was not the scholasticism of the sixteenth and seventeenth centuries he selected but that of the thirteenth.

10. Piet Fransen, "Sacraments: Signs of Faith," *Readings in Sacramental Theology*, ed. C. Stephen Sullivan (Englewood Cliffs: Prentice Hall, 1964) 62. Emphasis in original.

11. Edward Schillebeeckx, *Christ the Sacrament of Encounter with God* (New York: Sheed and Ward, 1966) 83.

12. In IV Sent., d.15,q.1,a.3,sol.3 ad 2; ibid.,d.6,q.1,a.3,sol.2; ibid.d.4,q.3,a.3,qc.4,obj.1.

13. Cf. ST,III,q.62,a.1.

14. See Lawler, *Symbol and Sacrament* 29–36.

15. Fransen, "Sacraments: Signs of Faith" 63.

16. Cf. Colman O'Neill, "The Role of the Recipient and Sacramental Signification," *Thomist* 21 (1958) 257–301, 508–540.

17. Ibid., 275–76. Emphasis in original.

18. Obvious difficulties with such an approach arise in the baptism of infants. But the baptism of adults, not the baptism of infants, is the paradigm for sacramental baptism. The baptism of infants is an exception to the general rule. For one solution to such difficulties, see O'Neill 276–296.

19. ST,III,49,3 ad 1.

20. See "Propositions on the Doctrine of Christian Marriage," Richard Malone and John R. Connery, eds., *Contemporary Perspectives on Christian Marriage* (Chicago: Loyola University Press, 1984) 15,19–21.

21. It is of note here that Can. 1099,2 of the 1917 *Code of Canon Law* exempted those who were baptized but never raised in the faith from the canonical form prescribed by Can. 1094. Pius XII abrogated this prescription on August 1, 1948, not because it was considered incorrect, but because it was considered too difficult to determine levels of Catholic upbringing and levels of nonfaith. What is of supreme interest here, however, is not that or why the prescription was abrogated, but that the necessity of personal faith for Catholic, sacramental marriage was part of Catholic law for thirty undisturbed years.

22. See *Epist.98,5*, PL 33,362; ST,III,68,9.

23. Edward Schillebeeckx, *Jesus: An Experiment in Christology* (New York: Seabury, 1979) 438.

24. "Sacramental Questions: The Intentions of Minister and Recipient," *Concilium* 31 (1967) 130.

25. AAS 55 (1963) 848.

26. G. Martelet, "Sixteen Christological Theses on the Sacrament of Marriage," *Contemporary Perspectives*, 279.

27. Juan Alfaro, "Faith," *Sacramentum Mundi: An Encyclopedia of Theology* (New York: Herder, 1968) 2:315.

28. L. Orsy, "Faith, Sacrament, Contract and Christian Marriage: Disputed Questions," in *TS* 43 (1982) 385.

29. "Sacramental Questions," 130.

30. "Propositions on the Doctrine of Christian Marriage," 2,3. My interpolation and emphasis.

31. IV Sent.,d.6,q.1,a.3 ad 5.

32. "Propositions on the Doctrine of Christian Marriage," 2,3.

33. "Faith and the Sacrament of Marriage," *Irish Theological Quarterly* 52 (1986) 172–173.

34. See Michael G. Lawler, "Faith, Contract and Sacrament in Christian Marriage," in *TS* 52 (1991) 712–731.

35. Susan Wood, "The Marriage of Baptized Non-Believers: Faith, Contract and Sacrament," *TS* 48 (1987) 294.

36. ST,I–II,59,1.

37. ST,I–II,49,1 and 3.

38. ST,III,69,4.

3

The Sacrament of Marriage: Biblical Basis

We have completed our consideration of the meanings of both marriage and sacramental marriage as they are understood in the tradition of the Catholic Church. We now begin our consideration of the origin and historical development of those meanings. In this chapter, we consider their foundation in "the Book," *ho biblos,* the Bible, which has been such a stable foundation for the religious meanings of the Christian Churches.

Marriage in the Old Testament

The Old Testament teaching on marriage, and indeed on all other matters, should be situated in the context of the Near Eastern cultures with which the biblical peoples had such intimate links. It is not my intention here, because it is not necessary to my purpose, to dwell at length on these cultures and their approach to marriage. They were all quite syncretistic, and a brief overview will provide a sufficient sense of both the general context and its specific distinctions from what we find in the Jewish-Christian Bible.

Underlying the themes of sexuality, fertility, and marriage in the cultures surrounding Israel are the archetypal figures of the god-father and the goddess-mother, the sources of universal life in the divine, the natural and the human spheres. Myths celebrated the marriage, the sexual intercourse and the fertility of this divine pair, legitimating the marriage, the intercourse and the fertility of every earthly pair. Rituals acted out the myths, establishing a concrete link between the divine and the earthly worlds and enabling men and women to share in, not only the divine action, but also the efficacy of that action. This is especially true of sexual rituals, which bless sexual intercourse and ensure that the unfailing divine fertility is shared by plants and animals and wives, all important elements in the male struggle for survival in those primitive cultures.

The Hebrew view of sexuality, marriage and fertility makes a radical break with this polytheistic perspective. The Old Testament, whose view of marriage I do not intend to treat fully here but only to the extent that it provides the basis for the New Testament view of marriage between Christians, does not portray a god-goddess couple, but only the Lord Yahweh who led Israel out of Egypt and is unique (Deut 6:4). There is no goddess associated with Yahweh, for the Lord Yahweh creates merely by uttering a creative word. At the apex of Yahweh's creation is *'adam*, man and woman together: "male and female he created them and he named them *'adam*" (Gen 5:2).

This fact alone, that Yahweh names male and female together *'adam*, that is, earthling or human, founds the equality of man and woman as human beings. In their pastoral response to the concerns of women in the church, the Catholic Bishops of the United States underscore this equality, insisting that women and men are equal in human dignity and favor with God. Will and Willma are equal in everything that is human; they are "bone of bone and flesh of flesh" (Gen 2:23). It is, in fact, only because they are equal that they can marry and become "one body" (Gen 2:24). These ideas are taken from the early Yahwist creation account. But the later Priestly account, which we find in the first chapter of Genesis, also records the creation of *'adam* "in the image of God . . . male and female" (1:27).

Equal man and woman, with their separate sexualities and fertilities, do not derive from a divine pair whom they are to imitate. They are called into being by the creative action of the sovereign God. Man and woman, *'adam*, their sexuality, their marriage, their fertility are all good, because they are the good gifts of the Creator God. Later Christian history, as we shall see, will have recurring doubts about the goodness of sexuality and its use in marriage, but the Hebrew tradition had none. As gifts of the Creator God, who "saw everything that he had made and behold it was very good" (Gen 1:31), sexuality, marriage and fertility were all good, and belonged to man and woman as their own, not as something derived from some divine pair.

When looked at within this context of creation-gift, all acquired a deeply religious, almost a sacramental, significance in Israel. That is not to say that they were sacred in the sense in which the fertility cults interpreted them as sacred, namely, as participation in the sexuality and sexual activity of the divine pair. In that sense they were not sacred, but quite secular. In another sense, however, the sense that they were from God and linked man and woman to God, they were both sacred and religious. "It was not the sacred rites that surrounded marriage that made it a holy thing. The great rite which sanctified marriage was God's act of creation itself."[1] It was God alone, unaided by any partner, who not only created *'adam* with sexuality and for marriage but also blessed him and her, thus making them inevitably good.

Man and woman together are named *'adam*. They are equal in human dignity and complementary to one another; there is no full humanity without both together. Human creation, indeed, is not complete until man and woman, Will and Willma, stand together as equals. Precisely because man and woman are equal, because they are *'adam*, because they are "bone of bone and flesh of flesh," that is, because they share human strengths and weaknesses, they may marry and become "one body" (Gen 2:24). Among the birds of the air and the animals of the field there "was not found a helper fit" for *'adam* (Gen 2:20), and it is not difficult to imagine man's cry of delight when confronted by woman. Here, finally, was one who was his equal, one whom he could marry and with whom he could become one.

That man and woman become one body in marriage has been much too exclusively linked in the western tradition to one facet of marriage, namely, the sexual. That facet is included in becoming one body, but it is far more than this. For body implies the entire person. "One personality would translate it better, for 'flesh' in the Jewish idiom means 'real human life.' "[2] In marriage a man and a woman enter into a fully personal union, not just a sexual or genital one. In such a union they become one social person and life, so complementing one another that they become *'adam*. They enter into a union which establishes not just a legal relationship, but a blood relationship which makes them one person. Rabbis go so far as to teach that it is only after marriage and the union of man and woman into one person that the image of God may be discerned in them. An unmarried man, in their eyes, is not a whole man. The mythic stories, interested as always in aetiology, the origin of things, proclaim that it was so "in the beginning," and that it was so by the express design of God. There can be for a Jew and for a Christian, no greater foundation for the human and religious goodness of sexuality, marriage, and fertility. Nor could there be a secular reality better than marriage for pointing to God and his steadfast loving relationship with Israel.

Central to the Hebrew notion of their special relationship with God was the idea of the covenant. The Deuteronomist reminded the assembled people: "You have declared this day concerning you that you are a people for his own possession" (Deut 26: 17-19). Yahweh is the God of Israel;

Israel is the people of Yahweh. Together Yahweh and Israel form a communion of salvation, a communion of grace, a communion, one could say, of one body. It was probably only a matter of time until the people began to image this covenant relationship in terms drawn from marriage and, as we saw earlier, it was the prophet Hosea who first did so. He preached about the covenant relationship of Yahweh and Israel within the biographical context of his own marriage to a harlot wife, Gomer. To understand his preaching, about both marriage and the covenant, we must first understand the times in which Hosea lived.

Hosea preached around the middle of the eighth century B.C.E., at a time when Israel was well established in Canaan. Many Israelites thought, indeed, that the former nomads had become too well adapted in their promised land, for as they learned their new settled ways they learned also a new cult of the fertility god, Baal. This cult, which seriously challenged their worship of Yahweh, was situated in the classic mold presented earlier, that of the god-goddess pair, with Baal as the Lord of the earth and Anat as his wife (and sometime sister). The sexual intercourse and fertility of these two were believed to establish the pattern of the fertile intercourse of every human pair, and this belief was acted out in worship as ritual sexual intercourse. Such sexual rituals were prohibited in the cult of Yahweh (Deut 23:18), and any Jewish woman participating in them was regarded as a harlot. It was such a harlot, Gomer, that Yahweh instructed Hosea to take for his wife (1:2-3).

It is quite irrelevant to our discussion whether the book of Hosea tells us what Hosea did in historical reality, namely, took a harlot-wife and remained faithful to her despite her infidelity to him, or whether it offers a parable about marriage as steadfast covenant. The only thing that is relevant is that Hosea found in marriage, either in his own marriage or in marriage in general, an image in which to represent for his people the steadfastness of Yahweh's covenantal love for them. On a superficial level, the marriage of Hosea and Gomer is like many another marriage. But on a more profound level, it serves as prophetic symbol, proclaiming, revealing and celebrating in representation the covenant relationship between Yahweh and Israel.

The names of Hosea's two younger children reflect the sad state of that relationship: a daughter is Not Pitied (1:6), and a son is Not My People (1:9). As Gomer left Hosea for another, so too did Israel abandon Yahweh in favor of Baal and become Not Pitied and Not My People. But Hosea's remarkable reaction proclaims and makes explicit in representation the remarkable reaction of Yahweh. He buys Gomer back (3:2); that is, he redeems her. He loves her "even as Yahweh loves the people of Israel, though they turn to other gods" (3:1). Hosea's action towards Gomer reveals in representation Yahweh's unfailing love for Israel. In both cases, that of the human marriage symbol and of the divine covenant symbolized, the one-body relationship had been damaged. But Hosea's action and reaction both models and is modeled on Yahweh's.

As Hosea has pity on Gomer, so Yahweh "will have pity on Not Pitied," and will "say to Not My People 'you are my people,' " and they will say to him, "Thou art my God" (2:23). The covenant union, that between Hosea and Gomer as well as that between Yahweh and Israel, is restored. A sundering of the marital covenant relationship is not possible for Hosea because he recognized that his God is not a God who can abide the dissolution of covenant, no matter what the provocation. He believed what the prophet Malachi would later proclaim: "I hate divorce, says Yahweh, the God of Israel . . . so take heed to yourselves and do not be faithless": (2:16).

There are two possibilities of anachronism to be avoided here. The first is that overworked word love. I have presented it as meaning an act of the will wishing well to another. In contemporary usage, it always means a strong affection for another person, frequently a passionate affection for a person of the opposite sex. When we find the word in our Bible, it is easy to assume without reflection that it means exactly these same things. It does not, at least not exclusively. The covenant love of which Hosea speaks is not a love of interpersonal affection. It is a willed love that is "defined in terms of loyalty, service and obedience."[3] When we read, therefore, of Hosea's steadfast love for Gomer and of Yahweh's faithful love for Israel, we ought to understand willed loyalty, service and obedience, not exclusively interpersonal affection.

The second possibility of anachronism rests in the hatred of divorce proclaimed by Malachi. "In the circumstances addressed by Malachi, what God hates is the divorce of Jew and Jew; there is silence about the divorce of Jew and non-Jew."[4] The post-exilic reforms of Ezra and Nehemiah mandate the divorce of all nonJewish wives and marriage to Jewish ones. Malachi speaks for this period. The divorce of Jewish wives is hated; the divorce of non-Jewish ones is obligatory. As we shall see, Paul will adapt this strategy to the needs of his Corinthian Church, and it continues to be a crucial factor in Catholic marital strategy in our day.

What ought we to make of the story of marriage that Hosea leaves to us? There is first a clear meaning about Yahweh: God is faithful. There is also a second, and somewhat more mysterious, meaning about marriage. Not only is it, on one level, the intimate communion of a man and a woman, but it is, on another level, also a prophetic symbol, proclaiming and revealing in representation the steadfast love of Yahweh for Israel. First articulated by the prophet Hosea, such a view of marriage recurs again in the prophets Jeremiah and Ezekiel. Ultimately, it yields the view of marriage between Christians that we find in the New Testament.

Both Jeremiah and Ezekiel present Yahweh as having two wives, Israel and Judah (Jer 3:6-14), Oholah-Samaria and Oholibah-Jerusalem (Ezek 23:4). Faithless Israel is first "sent away with a decree of divorce" (Jer 3:8), but that does not deter an even more faithless Judah from "committing adultery with stone and tree" (Jer 3:9). Israel and Judah are as much the harlots as Gomer but Yahweh's faithfulness is as unending as Hosea's. He offers a declaration of undying love: "I have loved you with an everlasting love; therefore, I have continued my faithfulness to you" (Jer 31:3; cf. Ezek 16:63; Isa 54:7-8). The flow of meaning, as in Hosea, is not from human marriage to divine covenant, but from divine covenant to human marriage. The belief in and experience of covenant fidelity creates and sustains the belief in and the possibility of fidelity in marriage, which then and only then becomes a prophetic symbol of the covenant. Yahweh's covenant fidelity becomes a characteristic to be imitated, a challenge to be accepted, in every Jewish marriage. Malachi's proclamation puts it in a nutshell: "I hate divorce, says Yahweh . . . so do not be faithless" (2:16).

Marriage in the New Testament

The conception of marriage as a prophetic symbol, a symbolic representation of a mutually faithful covenant relationship is continued in the New Testament. There is, however, a change of *dramatis personae*, from Yahweh-Israel to Christ-Church. Rather than presenting marriage in the then classical Jewish way as a symbol of the covenant union between Yahweh and Israel, the writer of the letter to the Ephesians presents it as an image of the relationship between the Christ and the new Israel, his Church. This presentation is of such central importance to the development of a Christian view of marriage, and unfortunately has been used to sustain such a diminished Christian view, that we shall have to consider it here in some detail.

The passage in which the writer offers his view of marriage (5:21-33) is situated within a larger context (5:21-6:9), which sets forth a list of household duties that exist within a family in his time and place. This list is addressed to wives (5:22), husbands (5:25), children (6:1), fathers (6:4), slaves (6:5) and masters (6:9). All that concerns us here is, of course, what is said to wives and husbands. There are two similar lists in the New Testament, one in the letter to the Colossians (3:18-4:1), the other in the first letter of Peter (2:13-3:7). But the Ephesians' list is the only one to open with a strange injunction. "Because you fear Christ subordinate yourselves to one another,'' or "give way to one another in obedience to Christ,'' or, in the weaker translation of the Revised Standard Version, "be subject to one another out of reverence for Christ.'' This injunction, commentators agree, is an essential element of what follows.

The writer takes over the household list from traditional material, but critiques it in 5:21. His critique challenges the absolute authority of any one Christian group over any other, of husbands, for instance, over wives, of fathers over children, of masters over slaves. It establishes a basic attitude required of all Christians, an attitude of giving way or of mutual obedience, an attitude which covers all he has to say not only to wives, children and slaves, but also to husbands, fathers and masters. Giving way is an attitude demanded of all Christians, because their fundamental attitude is that they "fear Christ.'' That phrase will ring strangely in pious ears, clashing with the deeply rooted claim that the basic attitude toward the Lord of the New Testament is not one of fear but of love. It is probably for this reason that the Revised Standard Version rounds off the rough edge of the Greek *phobos* and renders it as *reverence. Phobos*, however, does not mean reverence. It means fear, as in the Old Testament aphorism, the fear of the Lord is the beginning of wisdom (Prov 1:5; 9:10; 15:33; Ps 111:10).

The apostle Paul is quite comfortable with this Old Testament perspective, twice using the phrase *fear of God* in his second letter to the Corinthians (5:11 and 7:1). The latter would seem to be a better parallel for the passage in Ephesians. Second Corinthians 6:14-18 recalls the initiatives of God in the covenant with Israel and applies these initiatives to Christians, who are invited to respond with holiness "in the fear of God'' (7:1). The fear of God that is the beginning of wisdom is a radical awe and reverence that grasps the mighty acts of God and responds to them with holiness. In 2 Corinthians 6:14-17 that holiness is specified as avoiding marriage with unbelievers; in Ephesians 5:21 it is specified as giving way to one another. That mutual giving way is required of all Christians, even of husbands and wives as they seek holiness together in marriage, and even in spite of traditional cultural relationships which permitted husbands to lord it over their wives.

As Christians have all been admonished to give way to one another, it comes as no surprise that a Christian wife is to give way to her husband, "as to the Lord'' (5:22). What does come as a surprise, at least to the ingrained male attitude that sees the husband as supreme lord and master of his wife (and appeals to Ephesians 5:22-23 to ground and sustain that unChristian attitude), is that a husband is to give way to his wife. That follows from the general instruction that Christians are to give way to one another. It follows also from the specific instruction given to husbands. That instruction is not that "the husband is the head of the wife" in the way which males prefer to read and cite it, but rather that *"in the same way* that the Messiah is the head of the church is the husband the head of the wife."

A Christian husband's headship over his wife is an image of, and totally exemplified by, Christ's headship over the Church. When a Christian husband understands this, he will understand the Christian responsibility he assumes toward the woman-gift he receives in marriage as his wife. In a marriage between Christians, spouses are required to give way mutually, not because of any inequality between them, not because of any subordination of one to the other, not because of human fear, but only because they seek to live in service of one another as Christ lived in service of the Church. Will and Willma's mutual giving way and mutual obedience are no more than the total availability and responsiveness to one another required of best friends to become one body.

The way Christ exercises authority as we realized earlier, is set forth unequivocally in Mark 10:45: "The Son of Man came not to be served but to serve, and to give his life as a ransom (redemption) for many." *Diakonia*, service, is Christ's way of exercising authority; it was as a servant that "Christ loved the church and gave himself up for her" (5:25). A Christian husband, therefore, is instructed to be head over his wife by serving, giving way to, and giving himself up for her. Authority modeled on that of Christ does not mean control, giving orders, making unreasonable demands, reducing another person to the status of servant or, worse, of slave to one's every whim. It means service. The Christian husband-head, as Markus Barth puts it so beautifully, becomes "the first servant of his wife."[5] It is such a husband, and only such a one, that a wife is to hold in awe (v. 33b) as all Christians fear or hold Christ in awe (v.21b).

The reversal of verses 22 and 25 in verse 33 is interesting and significant. Verse 22 enjoined wives to be subject to their husbands and verse 25 enjoined husbands to love their wives. Verse 33 reverses that order, first commanding that husbands love their wives and then warmly wishing that wives fear their husbands. This fear is not fear of a master. Rather it is awe and reverence for loving service, and response to that love with one's own love-as-giving-way. Such love cannot be commanded by a tyrant. It is won only by a servant-lover, as the Church's love and giving way to Christ is won by a lover who gave, and continues to give, himself for her. This is the author's recipe for becoming one body: joyous giving way in response to, and for the sake of, love. It is a recipe echoed unwittingly by many a modern marriage counselor, though we need to recall that the love the Bible urges upon spouses is not exclusively interpersonal affection but willed loyalty, service, and obedience. That such love is to be mutual is clear from v.21, "Be subject to one another," though it is not stated that a wife is to love her husband. The reasons that the writer adduces for husbands to love their wives apply to all Christians, even to those called wives!

Three reasons are offered to husbands for loving their wives, all of them fundamentally the same. First of all, "husbands should love their wives as (for they are) their own bodies" (v. 28a); secondly, the husband "who loves his wife loves himself" (v. 28b); thirdly, "the two shall become one body" (v. 31b). There is abundant evidence in the Jewish tradition for equating a man's wife to his body. But even if there was no such evidence, the sustained comparison throughout Ephesians 5:21-33 between Christ-Church and husband-wife, coupled with the frequent equation of Church and body of Christ (1:22-23; 2:14-16; 3:6; 4:4-16; 5:22-30), clarifies both the meaning of the term body and the fact that it is a title of honor rather than of humiliation.

Love is always essentially creative. The love of Christ brought into existence the Church and made its believers "members of his body" (v. 30). In the same way, the mutual love of a husband and a wife creates such a union between them that, in the image of Christ and Church, she may be called his body and his love for her, therefore, may be called love for his body or for himself. But it is only within the creative and committed love of marriage that "the two shall become one body." Prior to marriage, a man did not have this body, nor did a woman have this head. Each receives a gift in marriage, a complement neither had before, which so fulfills each of them that they are no longer two persons but effectively one. For each to love the other, therefore, is for each to love herself or himself.

The second reason offered to a husband for loving his wife is that "he who loves his wife loves himself" (v. 28b; cf. v. 33a). Viewed within the perspective we have just elaborated, such reasoning makes sense. It makes even more Christian sense when we realize that it is a paraphrase of the great commandment cited by Jesus: "You shall love your neighbor as yourself" (Lev 19:18; Mark 12:21). Ephesians, of course, does not say that a husband should so love his wife. Where, then, is the link to the great commandment? It is provided through that most beautiful and most sexual of Jewish love songs, the Song of Songs. As noted before, in the Septuagint version the lover addresses his bride nine separate times as *plesion*, neighbor (1:9, 15; 2:2,10,13; 4:1,7;5:2; 6:4). "The context of the occurrence of *plesion* in the Song of Songs confirms that *plesion* is used as a term of endearment for the bride."[6] Other Jewish usage further confirms that conclusion, leaving no doubt that the author of Ephesians had Leviticus 19:18 in mind when instructing a husband to love his wife as himself.

The great Torah and Gospel injunction applies also in marriage: "you shall love your neighbor as yourself." As all Christians are to give way to one another, so also each is to love the other as himself or herself, including husband and wife in marriage. The paraphrase of Leviticus 19:18 repeats in another form what had already been said before in the own-body and the one-body images. What the writer concludes about the Genesis one-body image, namely, "This is a great mystery, and I mean in reference to Christ and the Church: (v. 32), will conclude our analysis of this central teaching of the New Testament on marriage.

"This is a great mystery," namely, as most scholars agree, the Genesis 2:24 text just cited. The mystery, as the Anchor Bible translation seeks to show, is that "this (passage) has an eminent secret meaning," which is that it refers to Christ and the Church. All that has gone before about Christ and the Church comes to the forefront here: that Christ chose the Church to be united to him, as body to head; that he loved the Church and gave himself up for her; that the Church responds to this love of Christ in awe and giving way. Christ who loves the Church, and the Church who responds in love, thus constitute one body, the Body of Christ (Eph 1:22-23; 2:14-16; 3:6; 4:4-16; 5:22-30), as Genesis 2:24 said they would. The writer is well aware that this meaning is not the meaning traditionally given to the text in Judaism, and he states this forthrightly. Just as in the great antitheses of the Sermon on the Mount Jesus puts forward his interpretations of biblical texts in opposition to traditional interpretations ("You have heard that it was said to the men of old . . . but *I* say to you"), so also here the writer asserts clearly that it is his own reading of the text ("*I* mean in reference to Christ and the church," v. 32b).

Genesis 2:24 was an excellent text for the purpose the writer had in mind, for it was a central Old Testament text traditionally employed to ordain and legitimate marriage. He acknowledges the meaning that husband and wife become one body in marriage; indeed, in v. 33, he returns to and demands that husband and wife live up to this very meaning. But he chooses to go beyond this meaning and insinuate more. Not only does the text refer to the union of husband and wife in marriage, but it refers also to that union of Christ and his church which he has underscored throughout Ephesians 5:1-33. On one level, Genesis 2:24 refers to human marriage; on another level, it refers to the covenant union between Christ and his Church. It is a small step to see human marriage as prophetic symbol of the covenant between Christ and his Church, and to see the communion between Christ and his Church as providing a model for human marriage and for the mutual conduct of the spouses within it.

Ephesians is not, of course, the only New Testament passage to speak of marriage and of the relationship between husband and wife. Paul does so in 1 Corinthians 7, apparently in response to a question which the Corinthians had submitted to him. The question was: "Is it better for a man to have no relations with a woman?" (7:1). The answer is an implied yes, but not an absolute yes. "Because of the temptation to sexual immorality, each man should have his own wife and each woman her own husband" (7:2). Marriage is good, even for Christians, he seems to say, as a safeguard against sexual sins, a point he underscores again in vv. 5-9. I do not wish to dwell, however, on this unenthusiastic affirmation of marriage. I wish only to highlight the equal relationship Paul assumes in marriage between a husband and a wife, a relationship he makes explicit in vv. 3-4. "The husband should give to the wife her conjugal rights, and likewise the wife to her husband. For the wife does not rule over her own body, but the husband does; likewise the husband does not rule over his own body, but the wife does."

A modern Christian might seize, as did medieval canonists seeking a precise legal definition of marriage, on Paul's dealing with marital intercourse as an obligation owed mutually by the spouses to one another. His contemporaries would have seized on something else, something astounding to them, namely, his assertion of strict equality between husband and wife in this matter. As Mackin puts it, correctly: "A modern Christian may wince at finding the apostle writing of sexual intercourse as an obligation, or even a debt, owed by spouses to one another, and writing of husbands' and wives' marital relationship as containing authority over one another's bodies. But Paul's contemporaries—at least those bred in the tradition of Torah and of its rabbinic interpreters—would have winced for another reason. This was Paul's assertion of equality between husbands and wives, and equality exactly on the juridical ground of authority and obligations owed."[7]

The author of 1 Timothy 2:8-15 also has something to say about the attitudes of men and women, laying down disproportionately what is expected of men (v. 8) and women (vv. 9-15). Of great interest in this text are the two traditional reasons he advances for the authority of men over women and the submission of women to men. The first is that Adam was created before Eve, and the other that it was Eve, not Adam, who was deceived by the serpent. Here the submission of women to men, and therefore of wives to husbands, of Willma to Will, is legitimated by collected stories of the mythical first human pair. For his part, the author of 1 Peter 3:1-6 requires that wives be submissive to their husbands "as Sarah obeyed Abraham" (v. 6). Such widespread views on such Old Testament bases were common in the Jewish world in which the Christian Church originated, which makes the attitude of the writer to the Ephesians all the more surprising.

The Old Testament passage that the writer of Ephesians chooses to comment on is one which emphasizes the unity in marriage of the first pair, and therefore of all subsequent pairs up to and including Will and Willma, rather than their distinction. He embellishes it not with Old Testament references to creation and to fall, but with New Testament references to the Messiah and to his love. This leads him to a positive appraisal of marriage in the Lord that was not at all customary in the Jewish and Christian milieu of his time. While he echoes the customary no to any form of sexual immorality (5:3-5), he offers a more-than-customary yes to marriage and sexual intercourse. For him marriage means the union of two people as one body-person, the formation of a new covenant pair, which is the gift of both God who created it and his Christ who established it in the love he has for the Church. Therefore, the marriage between a Christian man and a Christian woman becomes the prophetic symbol of the union that exists between Christ and the Church.

This doctrine does not mythicize marriage as an imitation of the marriage of some divine pair, nor does it idealize it beyond the capacity of Will and Willma to live it. Rather, it leaves marriage what it is, a human reality in which a man and a woman seek to become one person in a communion of life and love. What is added is only this simple and yet mysteriously complex: as they become one body-person in love, they provide through their marriage a prophetic symbol of a similar oneness that exists between Christ and the Church. Marriage is neither so secular a reality that Christ and Church cannot be represented by it, nor so base a union that it cannot become image and symbol of another, more mysterious union, nor so mythical a reality that women and men cannot live it together as one.

Qualities of Christian Marriage

The qualities of a marriage between Christian believers already appear from our biblical analysis. The root quality, the one that irradiates all the others, is the fulfillment of the great Torah and Gospel injunction: "You shall love your neighbor as yourself" (Lev 19:18; Mark 12:31; Matt 19:19). The Apostle Paul instructed the Romans that every other commandment was "summed up in this sentence, 'You shall love your neighbor as yourself' " (13:9). It is an instruction that holds true even, perhaps especially, in marriage. Love, of course, as I have already underscored, is a reality that is not easy to specify; I have uncovered a variety of different meanings. Here, however, I point out only that in marriage between Christians, in fulfillment of the great commandment, mutual love between the spouses is so radically necessary that the Supreme Marriage Tribunal of the Catholic Church, the Roman Rota, has ruled that, where love is lacking from the beginning, a marriage is invalid.[8] Mutual love, the judges ruled, is as critical in making a valid marriage as the traditional mutual consent.

We recall here that covenant love is a love defined in terms of loyalty, service, and obedience, not exclusively in terms of interpersonal affection. The Letter to the Ephesians specifies that the love demanded in a Christian marriage is that kind of love. It is, first, love as mutual giving way, love as mutual obedience or total availability. The love of Christian spouses in marriage is a love that "does not insist on its own way" (1 Cor 13:4), a love that does not seek to dominate and control the other spouse. Rather is it a love that seeks to give way to the other whenever possible, so that two persons might become one. The New Testament message proclaims that there is no place for self-centered individuals in marriage, least of all in a Christian marriage. That is not to say that there is no place in a marriage for individual differences. It is to say only that spouses who seek their own way always, who value the domination of their spouses, who never dream of giving way, will never become one person with anyone, perhaps not even with themselves.

In a Christian marriage, love requires not insisting on one's own way, but a mutual empathy with and compassion for the needs, feelings, and desires of one's spouse, and a mutual giving way to those needs, feelings, and desires when the occasion demands for the sake of, and in response to, love. In the final chapter, I shall discuss what the Greeks called *eros*, love that seeks its own good, and what they called *agape*, love that seeks the good of another, and I shall indicate how they may be productively allied in a Christian marriage. Here I state only that love that is exclusively *eros* is not the kind of love that leads two persons to become one body.

Love in a Christian marriage is, secondly, love as mutual service. All Christians are called to, and are sealed in baptism for, the imitation of Christ, who came "not to be served but to serve" (Mark 10:45). It cannot be otherwise in Christian marriage. In such a marriage there is no master, no mistress, no lady, no lord, but only mutual servants, each seeking to be of service to the other, so that each may become one in herself/himself and one also with the other. This is required not just because it is good general counsel for marriage, but specifically because Christian spouses are called in their marriage both to imitate Christ their Lord and to provide a prophetic symbol of his mutual servant-covenant with his Church. For Christian spouses, their married life is where they are to encounter Christ daily, there to be graced by him and come to holiness.

The love that constitutes Christian marriage is, finally, steadfast and faithful. The writer to the Ephesians instructs Will to love his wife "as Christ loved the church." We can be sure that he intends the same instruction also for Willma. Since Christ loves the Church as Hosea loves Gomer, steadfastly and faithfully, Will and Willma are to love each other steadfastly and faithfully. This mutually faithful love, traditionally called fidelity, makes sacramental marriage exclusive and permanent, and therefore an indissoluble community of love. I shall deal with the question of indissolubility in the concluding chapter of this book and, therefore, I shall content myself here by summarizing the conclusion reached there. Christian marriage is indissoluble because Christian love is steadfast and faithful and indissoluble. Indissolubility is a quality of Christian marriage because it is, first, a quality of Christian love. If marital love exists only inchoately as Will and Willma commit themselves one to the other on their wedding day, as it most surely does, then so also does the indissolubility of their marriage exist only inchoately.

Marital love, as mutual giving way, as mutual service, as mutual fidelity, as mainspring of indissoluble communion, is not a given in a Christian marriage; it is a task to be undertaken. Theologians say that it is an essentially eschatological task, a task about which spouses can always say: "already, but not yet;" already mutual love, but not yet steadfast; already mutual service, but not free of the desire to control; already one body, but not yet one blood person; already indissoluble in hope and expectation, but not yet in full reality; already prophetic representation of the covenant union between Christ and his Church, but not yet completely adequate representation. For authentic Christian spouses, marriage is always a challenge to which they are called to respond as disciples of the Christ they confess as the prophetic symbol of God.

Summary

This chapter can be summarized by four conclusions. First, marriage between humans is not an imitation of an eternal marriage between some divine couple, but a truly human reality which man and woman, *'adam*, hold as their own as gift from the Creator-God. In the giving and receiving of this gift, the Giver, the gift and the recipients are forever sacramentally bound. Secondly, this bond between Giver, gift and recipients is explicated by the prophet Hosea in his teaching that the marital communion between a man and a woman is the prophetic symbol of the covenantal communion between God and God's people. Thirdly, the writer of the letter to the Ephesians further explicates the symbolic nature of marriage by proclaiming a profound mystery, which is that as a man and a woman become one body-person in marriage, so also have Christ and his Church become one body-person, and that the one reflects the other. It is from such thinking that Catholic theologians will be led slowly to declare that *human* marriage may become, on occasion, also *Christian* sacrament. Fourthly, Christian marriage is a covenanted community of love between a man and a woman, love that does not seek its own, love that gives way, love that serves, love that is steadfastly faithful. Because it is both a covenant and a community of steadfast love, it is a permanent and exclusive state and a prophetic symbol of the steadfast covenant and love between Christ and his Church. That Christian marriage is such a reality, however, is not something that is simply so; rather it is something that is steadfastly to be made so. Permanence is not a static quality of marriage, but a dynamic quality of human love on which marriage, both secular and Christian, thrives.

Questions for Reflection

1. How would you explain the distinction between the ancient Jewish mythology of sexuality and marriage and that of the peoples surrounding them in the ancient Near East? Does that mythology make any contribution to the mythology you hold about sexuality and marriage?

2. Do you believe that sexuality and marriage are gifts from the Creator-God? If you do, is that enough for you to say that they relate you sacramentally to that God? If yes, in what sense?

3. Do you believe that marriage is sacramental? What does the word *sacramental* mean to you at this time?

4. The two great commandments in both Judaism and Christianity prescribe the love of God and the love of neighbor. According to the New Testament letter to the Ephesians, how are these commandments to be lived in a Christian marriage?

5. How do you understand the assertion that a man and a woman are to become one body in marriage? Is this one-body relationship a legal or a blood relationship? If it is a blood relationship, how would you go about getting a divorce?

NOTES

1. Edward Schillebeeckx, *Marriage: Secular Reality and Saving Mystery* (London: Sheed and Ward, 1965) 1:39.

2. F. R. Barry, *A Philosophy from Prison* (London: SCM, 1926) 151.

3. Moran, "The Ancient Near Eastern Background of the Love of God," 82.

4. Bruce J. Malina, *The New Testament World: Insights from Cultural Anthropology* (Atlanta: John Knox, 1981) 110.

5. Markus Barth, *Ephesians: Translation and Commentary on Chapters Four to Six.* The Anchor Bible (New York: Doubleday, 1974) 618.

6. J. Paul Sampley, *And the Two Shall Become One Flesh: A Study of Traditions in Ephesians 5:21-33* (Cambridge: University Press, 1971) 30.

7. Theodore Mackin, *What is Marriage?* (New York: Paulist, 1982) 56.

8. See Palmer, "Christian Marriage: Contract or Covenant" 647-648.

4

The Sacrament of Marriage: History

The doctrine of marriage in the preceding chapter was predominantly a Jewish doctrine, developed in the originating Jewish culture of the Christian movement. The developing Christian Church soon moved out of that Jewish culture into a Greco-Roman one in which Greek and Latin Fathers of the Church shaped the biblical doctrine about marriage within their own cultural context. To understand Christian marriage as it is conceived today, we must first seek to understand their teaching.

The Teaching of the Greek Fathers

We must keep in mind two things as we begin to consider the teaching of the Fathers. First, they reflect their times in their writings. We ought not to be surprised, then, when we find them saying things about men, women, and marriage that we would not say in our time. We ought not be surprised, for instance, when they assume that marriage is a union between two persons of quite unequal social value, a man who chooses a wife and a woman for whom her father chooses a husband. The early and anonymous Epistle to Diognetus portrays the general situation of these early Christians with respect to marriage. "Neither in region nor in tongue nor in the social institutions of life do Christians differ from other men. . . . They take wives as all do, and they procreate children, but they do not abort the fetus."[1] Second, because the teaching of the early Fathers was almost exclusively a defense of marriage against certain errors which threatened both its Christian value and its future, we find no systematic and full treatment of marriage as a social and Christian institution. The majority of these errors had Gnostic sources, and it will be to our benefit to consider, however briefly, the Gnosticism from which they came.

Gnosticism, a religious philosophy characterized by the doctrine that salvation is achieved through a special knowledge (*gnosis*), antedated Christianity and exercised a great influence on many Christian communities in the Mediterranean basin. Christian Gnostics came to look upon themselves as the only faithful interpreters of the Jesus movement. They disagreed with orthodox Christian teaching on two major points: first, they preached predestination, denying any free will to humans in either salvation or damnation; second, they preached a dualistic and pessimistic view of the world, a view in which good and evil are equally real. Both of these views affected their attitude toward marriage, and therefore the Fathers' expositions on marriage in reaction.

The most completely elaborated Gnostic teaching on predestination was perhaps that of the Roman Gnostic Valentinus. He taught that people are composed of three quite separate elements: matter (*hyle*), soul (*psyche*), and spirit (*pneuma*). Depending on which of these elements dominates in any given person, there results three quite different kinds of humans, hylics, psychics and pneumatics. Hylics, he taught, are predestined to damnation and are quite unredeemable: they constitute the majority of humanity. Pneumatics are predestined to salvation; they constitute a small minority of humanity, the true Gnostics. Psychics are evil, because soul is evil, but they can be saved by their free decision to participate in the *gnosis* of the Gnostics. Pneumatics, being spiritual and saved, are beyond anything that is material, and therefore disdain marriage and look upon it as evil.

Because matter was essentially evil, Gnostics believed, it could not have been created by a good God. That meant that Gnostics had to revise the classic Jewish-Christian approach to creation. That task was accomplished by Marcion, the son of the Bishop of Sinope. He taught that, of necessity, there had to be two gods, one the creator god who is the source of evil, the other the supreme god who is the source of goodness and salvation. The god who created evil is Yahweh, the god of the Old Testament; the supreme god is the Father of Jesus, who alone reveals him. The Old Testament, which reveals the evil deity, was created by hylics who have long since gone to their predestined damnation. It should be rejected, therefore, by the pneumatics, along with all its doctrines and its laws. Among such doctrines is the doctrine that men, women, and marriage were created good by God. Among such laws are those that legislate the relationships of men and women and their mutual sexual activity. Pneumatic Gnostics have risen above such laws and have no need to follow them. It is easy to see how such attitudes could generate, on the one hand, a negative ascetic approach to sexuality and marriage and, on the other hand, a licentious, permissive approach, known as antinomianism. The second and third century Fathers had to defend marriage against attacks on both these fronts.

By the middle of the second century of the Christian era, Alexandria had become established as the intellectual capital of the Hellenistic world. We would expect to find powerful Gnostics there, and our expectation is verified in the writings of the bishop of Alexandria, Clement. He tells us that there are the two kinds of Gnostics we have noted, namely, the kind who abstain from marriage and sexual intercourse because they believe them to be evil; and the antinomians who believe they are saved no matter what and are, therefore, above any law regarding sexuality and marriage.[2] He tells us of the ascetic Julius Cassianus whose work *On Continence* he cites: "Let no one say that because we have these members, that because the female is structured this way and the male that way, the one to give the seed and the other to receive it, that the custom of sexual intercourse is allowed by God. For if this structure were from God, toward whom we tend, he would not have pronounced blessed those who are eunuchs."[3]

Clement declares such an opinion "impious." His response is a simple one. There is only one God, and that God is good; marriage was created by the one God and, therefore, is good from its origin. "If marriage according to the law is sinful," he argues, "I do not see how anyone can say he knows God, and say that sin was commanded by God. But if the law is holy, marriage is holy. The apostle, therefore, refers this mystery to Christ and the Church."[4] Irenaeus of Lyons employs this same argument in his extensive refutation of the Gnostics. He mentions Marcion and Saturnius, "who are called the continent," and accuses them of frustrating the ancient plan of God and of finding fault with him "who made both male and female for the begetting of men."[5]

Those who attack sexuality and marriage as evil, Clement argues, attack the will of God and the mystery of creation, to which even the Virgin and Jesus were subject.[6] Marriage is primarily for procreation.[7] It is for something else, too, quite predictable in the culture of the time, namely, for a wife to bring help to her husband in the funding of his household, particularly in his sickness and old age.[8] It is finally a union in which "a pious wife seeks to persuade her husband, if she can, to be a companion to her in those things that lead to salvation."[9]

If the reply to the ascetic Gnostics was with an argument external to the nature of marriage, namely, marriage is good because it was created by God, the reply to the antinomians was based on what was taken to be the very nature of sexuality and, therefore, marriage. The antinomian posture may be exemplified in the teaching of Carpocrates, against whom both Clement and Irenaeus contend. He teaches that Jesus, the Son of

Joseph, escaped from the control of the creator of the world by a power he received from his father, the supreme God. After Jesus, those men who can attain the same power by knowledge can make the same escape. Since they have freed themselves from the powers of this world, and since they are predestined to salvation, they are freed also from the moral laws of this world and can engage in any kind of conduct without danger. Both Clement and Irenaeus accuse the antinomians of engaging in sexual immoralities, even in connection with the *agape* meal.[10] They counter the antinomian position with an appeal to the nature of sexuality as understood from sexual structure.

The early Greek Christian understanding of the nature of sexuality resembles that of the Stoic philosophers. It is most precisely represented in a statement from the Christian African, Lactantius. "Just as God gave us eyes, not that we might look upon and desire pleasure, but that we might see those actions that pertain to the necessity of life, so also we have received the genital part of the body for no other purpose than the begetting of offspring, as the very name itself teaches. This divine law is to be obeyed with the greatest of devotion."[11] This was a commonly accepted teaching, which carried with it several conclusions: first, by its very nature sexual intercourse is for the procreation of children; secondly, any such intercourse for purposes other than procreation is a violation of nature; and thirdly, any sexual intercourse when conception is impossible is a similar violation. From this established position Christian Fathers would argue that Gnostics, or anyone else, engaging in sexual intercourse for any purpose other than procreation were in violation of nature. It is an argument the Latin Church Fathers will continue to make into the twentieth century.

Already in the second century, in his apology for Christians, Justin had replied to Roman accusations about the sexual immorality of Christians by insisting that "either we marry only to have children or, if we do not marry, we are continent always."[12] But Clement goes much further, arguing that the only purpose for sexual intercourse is to beget a child and that any other purpose must be excluded. "A man who marries for the procreation of children," he argues, "must exercise continence, lest he desire his wife whom he ought to love, and so that he may beget children with chaste and moderated will. For we are not children of desire but of will."[13] Origen, his fellow Alexandrian, is just as clear, arguing that the man who has sexual intercourse only with his wife, "and with her only at certain legitimate times and only for the sake of children," is truly circumcised.[14] He underscores what he means by legitimate times, insisting that once a wife has conceived, intercourse is no longer good. Those who indulge in sexual intercourse with their own wives after they are already pregnant are worse than beasts, "for even beasts know that, once they have conceived, they do not indulge their mates with their largesse."[15]

The Teaching of the Latin Fathers

Two Latin Fathers advanced the Church's thinking on marriage and left it with a theology of marriage that became a given in Christian thinking for centuries afterwards. The lesser one is Tertullian, who wrote about marriage in both the orthodox Catholic and heretical Montanist periods of his life. In his first book, *To A Wife*, he exhibits the same ambivalence to sexuality and marriage that we have seen already in Origen. He grants that in the beginning marriage was necessary to populate the earth, but argues that when the end of the world is near there is no need for such activity. Paul may have allowed marriage as an antidote to lust, but Tertullian is in no doubt: "how much better it is neither to marry nor to burn (with concupiscence)." He will not even allow that marriage can be called good, for "what is *allowed* is not good . . . nor is anything good just because it is not evil."[16]

One would be excused for thinking that Tertullian has no time for marriage. But this same man, who is so pessimistic about marriage in his first book, in a second book under the same title writes the most beautiful lines on Christian marriage that one could ever hope to find. "What a bond is that of two faithful who are of one hope, one discipline, one service; both are brothers, both are servants. . . . They are truly two in one flesh, and where there is one flesh there is also one spirit. They pray together, they sleep together, they fast together, teaching one another, exhorting one another, sustaining one another."[17] One might conclude, with some legitimacy, that between his first and second books Tertullian had found a wonderful wife. When he became a Montanist, however, he regressed to his earlier judgment that Paul had simply allowed marriage which is, though not a sin, none the less a blot on a perfect Christian life.[18]

When we reach Augustine, the great Bishop of Hippo, we reach the systematic insight into the nature of marriage that was to mold and control the doctrine of the Latin Church down to our own day, so much so that Augustine is sometimes called the doctor of Christian marriage. His influence is always felt in talk about marriage. Pius XI, for instance, in the opening of his influential encyclical on Christian marriage *Casti Connubii*, turned to him as to the wellspring of the truths about Christian marriage to which the Catholic Church adheres. The Second Vatican Council also turned to him, developing its teaching about marriage within the schema of the threefold good of marriage as he described it (GS 48). Since

Augustine's influence on the doctrine of marriage is beyond doubt, we must look closely at it. His teaching must be viewed, however, in its context, a context which is again a defense against attack. As the Alexandrians defended sexuality and marriage against the attacks of the Gnostics, so did Augustine defend them against the attacks of the Manichees and Pelagians. We need to say a word, therefore, about these two.

The Manichees took their name from their founder, Mani, born in Babylonia about the year 216. Mani claimed to have received from an angel, at ages twelve and twenty-four, the definitive revelation about the nature of the world and of history. Here we need to consider only those aspects of Manicheeism which impinge on its teaching about marriage. First, it is a dualistic system, the dual opposites being good and evil, light and darkness, spirit and matter. Sexuality is listed among the dark and evil realities, along with wine and meat. Secondly, since Mani was looked upon as the ultimate prophet in the line of Jesus, he was said to have completed Jesus' teachings and to have organized the ultimate Church. That Church had two kinds of members, a group of the perfect and a group of auditors, those we would call today catechumens. The perfect always abstained from wine, meat, and sexual activity; the auditors abstained only on Sundays. It is not too difficult to guess what was the Manichean approach to sexuality and marriage. Both were evil in themselves and, therefore, to be avoided. Against this approach Augustine will repeat the argument of Clement and Irenaeus. Sexuality and marriage, created by God, are essentially good.

Pelagianism derived its name from a Briton, Pelagius, who lived in Rome around the year 380. The Pelagian attack against Augustine was led by a disciple of Pelagius, Julian, Bishop of Eclanum, rather than by Pelagius himself. The argument between Augustine and the Pelagians centered around the extent of our original fall from grace. Augustine taught that the original sin had seriously impaired human nature, so that after the Fall men and women could not do without grace what they had been able to do without it before the Fall. The Pelagians, on the other hand, taught that the Fall had left human nature unimpaired, so that men and women could do after the Fall what they had been capable of doing prior to the Fall without any help from grace. Against the Pelagians Augustine will teach that the results of the Fall make it very difficult to avoid sin in sexual intercourse, even in marriage. Pelagians, therefore, will accuse him of being a Manichee and of teaching that marriage and sexual intercourse are necessarily evil. They will be followed in this by many a modern writer who advert only to Augustine's anti-Pelagian writings. For such a complex writer, caught in the crossfire of two opposing heresies, that is too simplistic a procedure to be correct.

Augustine's basic statement about sexuality and marriage is ubiquitous, firm, and clear. Contrary to those Manichee heretics who hold that sexuality is evil and who condemn and prohibit marriage and sexual intercourse, he states that sexuality and marriage were created good by a good God and cannot lose that intrinsic goodness.[19] He specifies the good of marriage as threefold and insists that even after the Fall the marriages of devout Christians still contain this threefold good: fidelity, offspring, sacrament. "It is expected that in fidelity neither partner will indulge in sexual activity outside of marriage; that offspring will be lovingly accepted, kindly nurtured, and religiously educated; that in sacrament the marriage will not be dissolved and that neither partner will be dismissed to marry another, not even for the sake of offspring."[20] In this triple good Augustine intends the mutual fidelity of the spouses, the procreation of children, and indissolubility. Procreation has priority because "from this derives the propagation of the human race in which a living community is a great good."[21] And yet, to some extent at least, the good of sacrament is valued above the good of procreation, for he insists, as we have just seen, that a marriage cannot be dissolved, "not even for the sake of offspring." There may be here the seed of a Christian attitude to marriage that moves away from the social priority of procreation to the interpersonal priority of loving communion between the spouses, in the image of the loving communion between Christ and the Church. We shall see later that these two priorities have been given quite different weights at different times in Roman Catholic history, and that in the contemporary Roman Catholic approach they are given equal weights.

Alongside the tradition of the threefold good of marriage, Augustine advances yet another good, that of friendship between the sexes. In *The Good of Marriage*, after asserting that marriage is good, he gives an interesting explication of why it is good. "It does not seem to me to be good only because of the procreation of children, but also because of the natural companionship between the sexes. Otherwise, we could not speak of marriage in the case of old people, especially if they had either lost their children or had begotten none at all."[22] Later in the same work he returns to that idea. "God gives us some goods which are to be sought for their own sake, such as wisdom, health, friendship . . . others for the sake of friendship, such as marriage or intercourse, for from this comes the propagation of the human race in which friendly association is a great good."[23]

"In these passages," Mackin says, "Augustine has enriched the source whence Catholic canonists and theologians will later draw one of their 'secondary ends' of marriage . . . the *mutuum adiutorium* of the spouses, their mutual help, or support."[24] I believe he has done more. He has falsified in advance the claim of those who say that only in modern times has sexual intercourse and marriage been seen in relation to the relationship and love of spouses. But the source of what appears problematic in Augustine's teaching about marriage seems always to derive from what he says against the Pelagians. To this, therefore, we must now turn.

The basic position can be stated unequivocally, and there can be no doubt about it. Sexual intercourse between a husband and a wife, in Augustine's judgment, is a created good. It can, however, as can any good, be used sinfully. In the latter case, though, it is not the good itself which is sinful, but its disordered use. It is a balanced principle to which he will return at the end of his life in his *Retractions*. Evil and sin are never substantial, but are only in the will; there is, nevertheless, in men and women a concupiscence that causes sin. With the basic position in mind, it is not difficult to understand all that Augustine says about sexuality and marriage. Against the Pelagian, Julian, he explains carefully: "Evil does not follow because marriages are good, but because in the good things of marriage there is also a use that is evil. Sexual intercourse was not created because of the concupiscence of the flesh, but because of good. That good would have remained without that evil if no one had sinned."[25] It is clear that Augustine is saying there is one thing that is good, namely, sexual intercourse, and another thing that is evil, namely, concupiscence, that can transform good into evil. His position is much more nuanced than many notice: sexual intercourse is good in itself, but there are conditions under which it may be used evilly.

The condition under which it is good is the classic Stoic condition we have already seen in the Alexandrians, when it is for the begetting of a child. After the Fall, any other use, even between the spouses in marriage, is at least venially sinful. "Conjugal sexual intercourse for the sake of offspring is not sinful. But sexual intercourse, even with one's spouse, to satisfy concupiscence is a venial sin."[26] It is not sexual intercourse between spouses that is sinful, but only such intercourse controlled by concupiscence. Marital intercourse for the stoically natural reason, the procreation of children, is good. Intercourse as a result of concupiscence is sinful. By concupiscence he means the disordered pursuit by any appetite of its proper good, a pursuit which since the Fall is difficult to keep within the proper, reasonable limits. In effect, since the Fall of humanity and the rise of concupiscence, the sexual appetite is always threatened by concupiscence and, therefore, by sinfulness. It is not, though, the sexual appetite that is sinful; this is good. The Fathers of the Old Testament, he argues, took a "natural delight" in sexual intercourse and it was not sinful because it "was in no way given rein up to the point of unreasoning and wicked desire."[27] It is clear that disordered and unreasonable sexual intercourse fired by concupiscence is what Augustine considers sinful, not sexual intercourse per se. "Whatever, therefore, spouses do together that is immodest, shameful, filthy, is the vice of men, not the fault of marriage."[28]

Pope Gregory the Great shared Augustine's judgment that, because of the presence of concupiscence, even genital pleasure between spouses in the act of procreation is sinful. He went further and banned from access to the Church those who had just had pleasurable intercourse. "The custom of the Romans from antiquity," he explained, "has always been, after sexual intercourse with one's spouse, both to cleanse oneself by washing and to abstain reverently from entering the Church for a time. In saying this we do not intend to say that sexual intercourse is sinful. But because every lawful sexual intercourse between spouses cannot take place without bodily pleasure, they are to refrain from entering the holy place. For such pleasure cannot be without sin."[29] It is not difficult to see how such a doctrine could produce a strong ambivalence towards sexuality and marriage. That ambivalence weighed heavily in subsequent history on the theory and practice of Christian marriage.

The Scholastic Doctrine

Augustine's teaching controlled the approach to marriage in the Latin Church until the thirteenth century. The Scholastic theologians then made some significant alterations to it. Thomas Aquinas took over Augustine's three goods of marriage and transformed them, on the basis of his view of humanity, into the three ends of marriage. Thomas shared with Aristotle the view that humans, though sharing in the genus animal, were constituted by their reason a species apart from all other animals. This reason enables them to apprehend the ends proper to human animals, inscribed in the so-called natural law flowing from the design of the creator God. What were for the Neo-Platonic Augustine *goods* of marriage became for the Aristotelian Aquinas, therefore, *ends* of marriage, and ends established in a "natural" priority.

"Marriage," Aquinas argues, "has as its principal end the procreation and education of offspring . . . and so offspring are said to be a good of marriage." It has also "a secondary end in man alone, the sharing of tasks which are necessary in life, and from this point of view husband and wife owe each other faithfulness, which is one of the goods of marriage." There is another end in believers, "the meaning of Christ and church, and so a good of marriage is called sacrament. The first end is found in marriage in so far as man is animal, the second in so far as he is man, the third is so far as he is believer."[30] As is customary in Aquinas, this is a tight and sharply delineated argument, and its terminology *primary end—secondary end* came to dominate discussion of the ends of marriage in Roman Catholic manuals for seven hundred years. But neither the sharpness of the argument nor the authority of the author should be allowed to obscure the fact that it is also a very curious argument, for it makes the claim that the primary end of specifically *human* marriage is dictated by a man's generically *animal* nature. I intend to challenge this claim later.

Thomas, of course, wishes to insist always that reason must have control. Not that there is any rational control *in* the act of sexual intercourse, for animals lack reason. But there is reason *before* intercourse and, because there is, sexual intercourse between a husband and a wife is not sinful. The excess of passion which corrupts virtue (and which is, therefore, as in Augustine, sinful) is that which not only impedes reason, but also destroys it. Such is not the case with the intensity of pleasure in sexual intercourse for, "though a man is not then under control, he has been under the control of reason in advance."[31] Besides, nature has been created good by God, so that "it is impossible to say that the act in which offspring are created is so completely unlawful that the means of virtue cannot be found in it."[32]

There remains some ambivalence towards sexual desire, activity and pleasure. They are "occupations with lower affairs which distract the soul and make it unworthy of being joined actually to God."[33] But they are not sinful at all times and in all circumstances. Indeed, within the ends of marriage they are meritorious,[34] and Thomas asserts explicitly that to forego the pleasure and thwart the end would be sinful.[35] This latter opinion leads E. C. Messenger to go beyond Aquinas and declare that "both passion and pleasure are natural concomitants of the sex act, and so far from diminishing its goodness, if the sex act is willed beforehand according to right reason, the effect of pleasure and passion is simply to heighten and increase the moral goodness of the act, not in any way to diminish it."[36] That is an interesting opinion, quite defensible within Aquinas' system and quite in line, too, with Augustine's judgment about the "natural delight" taken in sexual intercourse by the Fathers of the Old Testament. It is also a far cry from Gregory, and a move toward both the liberation of marriage and legitimate sexual intercourse from any taint of sin and their recognition as a sign and a cause of grace, that is, as a sacrament.

The early Scholastics did not doubt that marriage was a sign of grace, but they did doubt that it was a cause of grace. They hesitated, therefore, to include it among the sacraments of the Church. Peter Lombard, for instance, defined sacrament in the categories of sign and cause. "A sacrament, properly speaking, is a sign of the grace of God and the form of invisible grace in such a way that it is its image and its cause. Sacraments are instituted, therefore, not only for signifying grace but also for causing it."[37] He proceeds to list the sacraments of the New Law, carefully distinguishing marriage from sacraments properly so called. "Some offer a remedy for sin and confer helping grace, such as baptism; others offer a remedy only, such as marriage; others support us with grace and virtue, such as eucharist and orders."[38] Marriage is a sacrament for Lombard only in the very general sense that it is a sign, "a sacred sign of a sacred reality, namely, the union of Christ and the church."[39]

It was the Dominicans, Albert the Great and Thomas Aquinas who firmly established marriage among the sacraments of the Church. In his commentary on Lombard, Albert lists the various opinions about the sacrament of marriage and characterizes as "very probable" the opinion which holds that "it confers grace for doing good, not just any good but that good specifically that a married person should do."[40] In his commentary on Lombard, Aquinas goes further, characterizing as "most probable" the opinion that "marriage, in so far as it is contracted in faith in Christ, confers grace to do those things which are required in marriage."[41] In his *Contra Gentiles*, he is even more positive, stating bluntly that "it is to be believed that through this sacrament [marriage] grace is given to the married."[42] By the time he wrote his completed thought in the *Summa Theologiae*, he lists marriage among the seven sacraments with no demur whatever about its grace-conferring qualities. The combined theological authority of Albert and Thomas ensured for marriage, albeit late in Christian history, a place among the sacraments of the Catholic Church. By the time of the Reformation the opinions of Albert and Thomas was held universally by theologians.

The Teaching of the Church

In the Middle Ages, under the banners of the Cathari and Albigenses, the Neo-Platonic and Gnostic dualism which the Fathers combated but never definitively put to rest enjoyed a period of resurgence. There was again a widespread suspicion and downright negative pessimism toward sexuality and marriage, and once again the Church intervened to defend these gifts of a good God. The Second Lateran Council (1139) condemned those who "condemn the bonds of legitimate marriage," and ordered them "to be coerced by external powers" to accept the goodness and legitimacy of marriage (DS 718). While talk of external coercion might make us wince today, we can still be glad of the convincing evidence it offers of how strongly the Church felt about the goodness of legitimate sexuality and marriage. Catharism was castigated further in the Council of Verona (1184) where, for the first time in a document of the Church, marriage was listed as a sacrament in the company of baptism, Eucharist and confession (DS 761). As part of the formula for healing the great schism between East and West, the Council of Lyons (1274) listed marriage among seven sacraments (DS 860), a listing repeated by the Council of Florence (1439), with the specification that these seven sacraments "both contain grace and confer it on those who receive them worthily" (DS 1310).

The concluding section of the Florentine decree deals explicitly with marriage, and is an excellent summary of everything that had been taught about it until then. "The seventh sacrament is marriage, which is a sign of the union between Christ and his church. . . . A triple good is designated for marriage. The first is offspring accepted and raised to worship God; the second is fidelity, in which each spouse ought to serve the other; the third is the indivisibility of marriage because it signifies the indivisible union of Christ and Church. And, although separation is permissible in the case of fornication, remarriage is not, for the bond of legitimately contracted marriage is perpetual" (DS 1327). That marriage is a sacrament, that it contains and confers grace, that it is indissoluble, all these are now established doctrines in the western Church. When the Council of Trent teaches them in response to the Reformers, it is not inventing, but merely stating, the established doctrine and faith of the Church. I see no need to go over that ground again. There is one decision Trent made about marriage, though, that I must reflect on, because in its time it was an important and innovative response to a pressing problem. I refer to the decree *Tametsi*, which sought to eliminate clandestine marriages by establishing a legal form without which marriage is not valid.

In a community of believers who hold that marriage is a sacrament, that it symbolizes the union of Christ and his Church, confers grace on those who receive it worthily, and is indissoluble, a crucial question needs to be settled. It is an apparently simple, but in reality a very complex, question: *when* is there a sacramental marriage? At what precise moment in time are two persons sacramentally and indissolubly married? This question vexed Latin lawyers and, to a lesser extent, theologians for centuries, for in the western tradition it had two quite differing answers.

As noted earlier, there was the Roman answer: consent between a man and a woman makes marriage. There was the northern European answer: sexual intercourse between a man and a woman after the giving of consent makes marriage. Both answers, of course, had long cultural histories, each with good reasons why it should be so. When the Church, then, came to formulate an answer to the question of what really makes an indissoluble marriage, there were proponents on both sides. I do not intend to detail the resulting discussions, since for the purposes of this book they have only tangential interest.[43] All I need to do here is outline what came to be the final solution.

By the middle of the twelfth century, the lines of the consent or intercourse debate had taken clear shape, the theologians of the University of Paris championing the Roman tradition, and the canonists of the University of Bologna the European. The Master at Bologna in the mid-twelfth century was Gratian, who around 1140 completed a work of collecting and harmonizing all the texts of marriage available to him at the time. The work, usually known simply as *Gratian's Decree*, sought to offer a solution to the problem of consent or intercourse by combining the two, employing a distinction already introduced by his Parisian opponents.

That distinction was between initiated marriage and completed marriage, and Gratian employed it to harmonize the two divergent opinions. Consent initiates a marriage; subsequent sexual intercourse ratifies and consummates it. "It should be known that marriage is initiated by betrothal (consent), perfected by sexual intercourse. Therefore, between spouses there is marriage, but only initiated; between spouses who have engaged in sexual intercourse, there is ratified marriage."[44] This compromise opinion ultimately passed into the law of the Roman Church, and was enshrined in its Code of Canon Law in the twentieth century as a distinction between ratified marriage and ratified and consummated marriage, that is, marriage ratified by the Church and completed by the spouses in their sexual intercourse.[45]

To Will and Willma such intricacies probably appear as so much indelicate nit-picking. "We love one another" seems to them a sufficient answer to almost any question. But the history of clandestine marriages shows that, at the time, it was anything but nit-picking. A clandestine marriage is one that is contracted by the simple exchange of consent between a man and a woman without any publicity or any witnesses. By the late Middle Ages such marriages had become a scourge in Europe. They took place between couples who could not marry publicly because their parents would not allow it, or because a class distinction forbade it, or because of countless other reasons. Unfortunately, after a time, many such marriages came to a litigated end, with charge and countercharge of concubinage, fornication, and illegitimacy.

The Roman opinion acknowledged the validity of such marriages, for consent makes marriage; the European opinion acknowledged the validity of such marriages when they were consummated; after Gratian, the Roman Church acknowledged the indissolubility of such consummated marriages. That such indissoluble marriages, sacraments of the unending union between Christ and the Church, would simply cease to be at someone's unsubstantiated whim was intolerable for the Church. Already in the ninth century, the eastern Church had tried to put an end to clandestine marriages, the Emperor Leo IV decreeing that any attempt to marry without ecclesiastical witnesses rendered the marriage null. In the sixteenth century the western Church tried to proscribe them, the Council of Trent decreeing in *Tametsi* that a true and valid marriage, one that the Church would recognize as sacramental and indissoluble, must be celebrated publicly in the presence of a duly appointed priest and two witnesses (DS, 1813–1816). Only if celebrated in this form, as it came to be called, would a marriage be recognized as valid.

Tametsi transformed marriage from a simple contract, one not restricted by any external legal requirements, to a solemn contract, one in which certain legal formalities had to be met for the contract to be valid. That transformation required a parallel transformation in the form in which the sacrament of marriage was celebrated, but that change was only in the externals of the celebration and not in the substance of the sacrament. After *Tametsi*, as before, the sacrament of marriage is still constituted by the consent of the man and the woman, and the marriage is constituted indissoluble by their subsequent intercourse. The change introduced by Trent's decree was well within the powers of the Church to make, and it is similarly within its power to make any analogous change today in the externalization of the man's and woman's giving of consent. I shall return to this point later.

Three years after the Council of Trent, in 1566, Pope Pius V authorized the publication of a *Catechism of the Council of Trent*, which contained teaching on the sacrament of marriage of interest to us. It defined marriage as a "conjugal union of man and woman between legitimate persons, which is to last throughout life"; it taught that marriage "is not a simple donation but a mutual contract"; it listed three goods of marriage, "offspring, faith and sacrament," insisting on the primacy of the first over the others.[46] For the next four hundred years, in an attempt to define the juridical essence of marriage, canon lawyers ignored the first of these notions to concentrate exclusively on the other two. We now inquire how that happened and what it means.

The Modern Period

Gratian's *Decree* laid a basis for the codification of the laws of the Catholic Church. That process, which took seven hundred years to come to fruition, achieved its goal under the editing of Cardinal Pietro Gasparri in the *Code of Canon Law*, promulgated on Pentecost Sunday, 1917. Title VII of Book Three of that *Code* relates to marriage, and is heavily inspired by Gasparri's influential book on marriage, *Tractatus Canonicus de Matrimonio*, published in 1892. Three notions were prominently developed in that book: marriage is a contract; the formal object of the contract is the permanent and exclusive right of the spouses to each other's bodies for sexual intercourse; the primacy of procreation over the other ends of marriage. These three notions would control the Catholic Church's approach to marriage questions until the Second Vatican Council. We need to consider each briefly.

Even Gasparri himself acknowledged that marriage was never considered a contract in either Roman or European law. He insisted, however, that it must be a contract because it is formed by two parties mutually consenting to the same thing. David Fellhauer demonstrates that there is no official source "which presents the juridical essence of marriage as the *ius in corpus* (right to the body) for procreation or which identifies the object of consent in similar terms."[47] In an equally comprehensive analysis, Urban Navarette points out that, in the documents of the Church and in the corpus of canon law itself, "we find hardly anything about the ends of marriage precisely as goals until the formulation of Canon 1013,1."[48] He points out further that a preliminary version of Canon 1013 indicated no hierarchy of ends and concludes that the 1917 *Code of Canon Law* is the first official document of the Catholic Church to embrace the terminology *primary end-secondary end*.

The opening canon on marriage firmly locates it as a contract (1012,1), and affirms the identity of contract and sacrament (1012,2). This latter assertion was the end point of a nineteenth century dispute between the Church and emerging European states about who had jurisdiction in marriage. By asserting the identity of contract and sacrament in the marriages of Catholics, the Church was asserting its authority over not only the sacrament of marriage but also over any marriage of Catholics. It was asserting also by implication that every marriage contract between two baptized Christians was also, by that very fact a sacrament. We shall consider that claim carefully in our concluding chapter.

The hierarchy of marital ends is asserted immediately following the establishment of marriage as contract and sacrament. "The primary end of marriage is the procreation and nurture of children; its secondary end is mutual help and the remedying of concupiscence" (Can.1013,1). This hierarchy of ends implies also a subordination of ends. Since the *ends*, no longer the Augustinian *goods*, of marriage are primary and secondary, in case of conflict the secondary end must always bow to the primary end. That subordinationism controlled all discussion of marital questions in the years that followed the promulgation of the Code. The ancient Roman opinion about what makes marriage is enthroned in the Code: marriage is created by the consent of the parties (Can. 1081,1). That consent "is an act of the will by which each party gives and accepts a perpetual and exclusive right over the body for acts which are of themselves suitable for the generation of children" (Can. 1081,2). So crucial is the consent, and specifically the consent to rights over the body, that absence of either invalidates an attempted marriage (Can. 1082, Can. 1086,2).

The 1917 *Code*, then, yields the following reductionist definition of both the contract and the sacrament of marriage which, remember, are inseparable in the marriages of baptized persons. Marriage is "a permanent society (Can.1082), whose primary end is procreation and nurture (Can. 1013), a society that is in species a contract that is unitary and indissoluble by nature (Can. 1012 and 1013,2), whose substance is the parties' exchanged rights to their sexual acts (Can. 1081,2)."[49] That definition articulates the essence of marriage that controlled the arguments in Catholic courts up to the Second Vatican Council, when it was displaced. I call it a reductionist definition because, while it carefully specifies what is included in the essence of marriage, it equally carefully specifies, at least by implication, what is left out. It was precisely on that basis that it was attacked and eventually replaced.

In December 1930, Pope Pius XI published an important encyclical on marriage, *Casti Connubii*. In it, predictably, he insisted on everything we have just considered as the juridical essence. But, unpredictably, he did more. He retrieved and gave a prominent place to that long ignored item from the *Catechism of the Council of Trent*, marriage as a union of conjugal love and intimacy. If Will and Willma consider only the juridical definition of marriage, they could easily conclude that marriage has nothing to do with mutual love, that they could be married even if they hated one another as long as each gave to the other the right over her or his body. By emphasizing the essential place of mutual love in a marriage, Pius firmly rejected such nonsense and placed the Catholic view of marriage on the track to a more personal definition.

Marital love, Pius teaches, does not consist "in pleasing words only, but in the deep attachment of the heart (will) which is expressed in action, since love is proved by deeds." This love proved by deeds "must have as its primary purpose that man and wife help each other day by day in forming and perfecting themselves in the interior life . . . and above all that they may grow in true love toward God and their neighbor."[50] So important is the mutual love and interior formation of the spouses, he continues, that "it can, in a very real sense, as the Roman Catechism teaches, be said to be the *chief reason and purpose of marriage,* if marriage be looked at not in the restricted sense as instituted for the proper conception and education of the child, but more widely as the blending of life as a whole and the mutual interchange and sharing thereof'' (emphasis mine). In these wise words, Pius directs us to see that there is more to the essence of marriage than can be contained in the precise canonical categories of the reductionist definition. European thinkers were poised to point in the same direction, most influentially two Germans, Dietrich Von Hildebrand and Heribert Doms.

In the opening paragraph of his work *Marriage*, Von Hildebrand states the problem precisely. The modern age, he suggests, is guilty of a terrible antipersonalism, ''a progressive blindness toward the nature and dignity of the spiritual person.'' This antipersonalism expresses itself in all kinds of materialism, the most dangerous of which is biological materialism which considers man as a more highly developed animal. ''Human life is considered exclusively from a biological point of view and biological principles are the measure by which all human activities are judged.''[51]

The juridical approach to marriage, with its insistence on rights over bodies and their physiological functions, is wide open to the charge of biological materialism. So, too, is the centuries old Stoic-cum-Christian doctrine that argues from biological structure to human ''nature'' and to ''natural'' ends. So, too, is Aquinas' position which founds the primary end of *human* marriage in the *biological* structure of men and women. In contrast to this biological approach, Von Hildebrand introduced a radical innovation in thinking about marriage, claiming Pius XI and *Casti Connubii* in support of his central thesis that marriage is for the building up of loving communion between the spouses. Conjugal love, he claims, is the primary meaning and ultimate end of marriage.[52]

In marriage, the spouses enter into an interpersonal relationship, in which they confront one another as I and Thou, as Ego and Other, and ''give birth to a mysterious fusion of their souls.''[53] This fusion of their very beings, not merely the biological fusion of their bodies, is what the oft-quoted ''one body'' of Genesis intends. It is this interpersonal fusion which is the primary meaning of the spouses' sexual intercourse, and intercourse achieves its end when it expresses and leads to such fusion. ''Every marriage in which conjugal love is thus realized bears spiritual fruit, becomes *fruitful*—even though there are no children.''[54] The parentage of such thought in modern personalist philosophy is as clear as the parentage of biological-natural thought in Stoic philosophy. Even clearer, though, is the deep resonance of such an interpersonal description of marriage and lovemaking with the lived experience of many married couples.

Doms agreed with Von Hildebrand that what is natural or unnatural for human animals is not to be decided on the basis of what is natural or unnatural for nonhuman animals. Humans are specifically spiritual animals, vitalized by a spiritual soul, and are not to be judged, as the Stoics and Aquinas judged them, on the basis of animal biology. Human sexuality is essentially the capacity and the desire to fuse, not only one's body, but also one's very self with another person. Sexuality drives a human to make a gift of herself or himself (not just of her or his body) to another, in order to create a communion of persons and lives which fulfills both. Within such a perspective, marital intercourse is a powerful, interpersonal activity in which a woman gives herself to a man and a man gives himself to a woman, and in which they accept the gift of each other, to express and create marital communion.

The primary end of sexual intercourse in this perspective is the marital communion between the spouses, a communion which is signified and created in intercourse. This primary end is achieved in every act of intercourse in which the spouses actually enter into intimate communion. Even in childless marriages, marriage and intercourse achieve their primary end in the marital communion of the spouses, their *two-in-oneness* as Doms would have it. He summarizes his case in a clear statement. "The immediate purpose of marriage is the realization of its meaning, the conjugal two-in-oneness. . . . This two-in-oneness of husband and wife is a living reality, and the immediate object of the marriage ceremony and their legal union." The union of the spouses tends naturally to the birth and nurture of new persons, their children, who focus the fulfillment of their parents, both as individuals and as a two-in-oneness. "Society is more interested in the child than in the natural fulfillment of the parents, and it is this which gives the child primacy among the natural results of marriage."[55]

The Church's immediate reaction to these new ideas, as has been so often the case in theological history, was a blanket condemnation, which made no effort to sift truth from error. In 1944, the Holy Office condemned "the opinion of some more recent authors, who either deny that the primary end of marriage is the generation and nurture of children, or teach that the secondary ends are not essentially subordinate to the primary end, but are equally primary and independent."[56] In 1951, as the opinions of Von Hildebrand and Doms persisted and attracted more adherents, Pius XII felt obliged to intervene again. The truth is, he taught, that "marriage, as a natural institution in virtue of the will of the creator, does not have as a primary and intimate end the personal perfection of the spouses, but the procreation and nurture of new life. The other ends, in as much as they are intended by nature, are not on the same level as the primary end, and still less are they superior to it, but they are essentially subordinate to it."[57] The terms of the problem could not be made more precise. The balance, however, was to be seriously shifted by the Second Vatican Council.

Before the Council opened, the bishops had been sent a preparatory schema on "Marriage, Family and Chastity." A consideration of the fate of that schema will introduce a contemporary Catholic theology of marriage and conclude this chapter. The schema had been prepared by a theological commission chaired by Cardinal Ottaviani, then prefect of the Holy Office, who explained that the schema laid out the "objective order . . . which God himself willed in instituting marriage and Christ the Lord willed in raising it to the dignity of a sacrament. Only in this way can the modern errors that have spread everywhere be vanquished."[58] Among these errors are "those theories which subvert the right order of values and make the primary end of marriage inferior to the biological and personal values of the spouses, and proclaim that conjugal love itself is in the objective order the primary end."[59] The schema highlights the primary end-secondary end terminology, the primary end being the procreation and nurture of children, the secondary end the mutual help of the spouses. The debate over the schema, both in the Central Theological Commission and, then, in the Council itself centered around the hierarchy of ends, specifically around the relative values of conjugal love and the procreation of children. For our purposes here, only the outcome of that debate, as it was promulgated in the *Church in the Modern World*, need be discussed.

We have already dealt with this material in chapter 2, and we need to consider it here only summarily to complete the conspectus of history. The Constitution describes marriage as a "communion of love" (GS 47), an "intimate partnership of conjugal life and love" (GS 48). The Council's position could not be clearer. In the face of demands to consign the conjugal love of the spouses to a secondary place, it declared that love to be of the very essence of marriage. There was another explicit rejection of Gasparri. Marriage, the Council declares, is founded in a "conjugal covenant of irrevocable personal consent" (GS 48). Gone is Gasparri's word *contract*, replaced by the biblical word *covenant*, situating marriage as an *interpersonal* rather than an exclusively *juridical* reality. This interpersonal characteristic is underscored by the choice, again in the face of demands to remain with the traditional characterization, of a way to characterize the formal object of the covenanting. The Council declares that the spouses "mutually gift and accept one another" (GS 48), rejecting the reductionist, material biological notion that they give merely the right to one another's bodies. In their mutual covenanting and gifting, Will and Willma create a communion of love which is permanent, which is to last for the whole of life.

The Council teaches that, of course, both marriage and the marital love of the spouses "are ordained for the procreation and education of children, and find in them their ultimate crown" (GS 48). But, again despite insistent voices to the contrary, it rejected the primary end-secondary end dichotomy. To make sure that its rejection was understood, the preparatory commission was careful to explain that the text just cited "does not suggest (a hierarchy of ends) in any way."[60] Marriage and conjugal love "are by their very nature ordained to the generation and education of children," but that "does not make the other ends of marriage of less account" (GS 50). Marriage "is not instituted solely for procreation" (GS 50). The intense debate which took place both in the preparatory commission and in the Council itself makes it impossible to claim that the refusal to speak of a hierarchy of ends in marriage was the result of oversight. It was the result of a deliberate and explicit choice of the Catholic Church meeting in Council. Any doubt was definitively removed by the appearance of the revised *Code of Canon Law* in 1983.

Marriage, the new *Code* decrees, is "brought into being by the lawfully manifested consent of persons who are legally capable" (Can 1057,1), but that consent "is an act of the will by which a man and a woman by irrevocable covenant mutually give and accept *one another* for the purpose of establishing a marriage" (Can 1057,2). The marriage that is established by covenant "is ordered to the well-being of the spouses and to the procreation and upbringing of children" (Can 1055,1), with no specification of either of these ends being primary or secondary. The Catholic Church changed its law to be in line with its theology of marriage, moving beyond the narrow juridical essence to embrace in the essence of marriage the mutual love and communion of the spouses.

The great Protestant theologian Karl Barth once complained that the traditional Christian doctrine of marriage, both Protestant and Catholic, situated marriage in juridical rather than in theological categories.[61] The Roman Catholic Church has now corrected that grave imbalance. I hope that is good news for Barth and for all married people. Even more importantly, I hope it will be good news for Will and Willma as they seek to live out their equal and intimate partnership of life and love, not only in marriage but more especially in the sacrament of marriage.

Summary

Three ideas from this chapter should be underscored. First, a very negative attitude toward sexuality and its use in marriage crept into Christianity from heretical Gnostic and Stoic sources. Though this attitude was combated consistently by theologians and Church councils, it remains rooted in the ongoing Christian ethos about marriage. Second, this negative attitude toward sexuality contributed to the enthronement, however implicit, of several judgments in the Catholic tradition. Among these are: marriage, involving sexuality and therefore somehow evil, cannot be a cause of grace, that is, cannot be a sacrament; virginity and celibacy are superior, and therefore preferable, to marriage; Holy Orders and those in Holy Orders are holier, and therefore superior, to marriage and those in marriage. These judgments have left their mark on the Roman Catholic tradition; they are quite nonsensical when measured against the biblical tradition elaborated in the preceding chapter. Finally, with the acceptance of Christian marriage as a sacrament, came the need to specify just when a sacramental marriage took place and was indissoluble. Gratian's distinction between initiated marriage, considered a fully valid but dissoluble marriage, and consummated marriage, considered a fully valid and indissoluble marriage, contributed an important response to that need. Trent's *Tametsi,* which decreed an entirely novel form without which Christians could enter neither a valid marriage nor a valid sacrament, contributed another. Gratian's distinction and Trent's form became inscribed in the canon law of the Roman Church and still, even after the substantive changes introduced by Vatican II, control answers to questions which arise about not only the legality and validity of marriage, but also about its sacrament. I shall challenge some of these questions and answers in the final chapter.

Questions for Reflection

1. In your judgment, does the negative attitude towards sexuality inherited from Gnosticism and Manicheeism still persist in Christianity? If it does, how does it manifest itself? How is it to be reconciled with the biblical doctrine that sexuality and marriage are creations of the good God and, therefore, good?

2. What exactly does the word *procreation* mean to you? What difference does it make whether procreation is said to be a good or an end of marriage? Where would the difference manifest itself in the marriage of Will and Willma?

3. Do you look upon marriage more as a contract or as a covenant? Can you clarify the differences?

4. The *Code of Canon Law*, which once described the object of the marriage contract as each spouse's right to the other's body, now describes it as the mutual gifting of persons. Does this shift from biological to personal emphasis diminish or enhance your view of Christian marriage? Please explain.

5. If theological theory undergoes a shift from describing the ends of marriage—the mutual love of the spouses and procreation—as primary and secondary, to describing them as equal, what concretely changes for Will and Willma—and for you?

NOTES

1. *Epist. ad Diognetum* 5,PG 2,1173.
2. *Stromatum* 3,5,PG 8,1143-1147.
3. Ibid., 3,13,PG 8,1191.
4. Ibid., 3,12,PG 8,1186.
5. *Adv.Haer.* 1,28,1,PG 7,690.
6. *Stromatum* 3,17,PG 8,1206.
7. Ibid., 2,23,PG 8,1086 and 1090. See also *Paed.* 2,10,PG 8, 498.
8. Ibid., 3,12,PG 8,1184 and 2,23,PG 8,1090-1091.
9. Ibid., 4,19,PG 8, 1333.
10. Ibid., 3,2,PG 8,1103-1111; *Adv.Haer.* 1,25,PG 7,680-686.
11. *Divinarum Institutionum* 6,23,PL 6,718.
12. *Apologia Prima* 1,29,PG 6,374.
13. *Stromatum*, 3,7,PG 8,1162.
14. *In Gen. Hom.* 3,6,PG 12,180.
15. Ibid., 5,4,PG 12, 192.
16. *Ad Uxorem I* 2-3,PL 1,1277-1279. My emphasis.
17. *Ad Uxorem II* 9,PL 1, 1302-1303.
18. *De Pudicitia* 16,PL 2, 2,1012.
19. *De Nupt. et Concup.* 2,32,54,PL 44,468-469. See also *De Bono Coniugali* passim,PL 40,374-396.
20. *De Gen. ad Litt.* 9,7,12,PL 34,397; also *De Bono Coniug.* 24,32,PL 40,394.
21. *De Bono Coniug.* 9,9,PL 40,380.
22. PL 40,375.
23. PL 40,380.
24. Mackin, *What Is Marriage?* 141.
25. *Contra Julianum* 3,23,53,PL 44,729-730.
26. *De Bono Coniug.* 6,6,PL 40,377-378; 10,11,PL 40,381.
27. Ibid., 16,18,PL 40,386.
28. Ibid., 6,5,PL 40,377.
29. *Epistolarum Liber IX* Epist 64,PL 77,1196.
30. ST III (Suppl.),65,1,c.
31. ST III (Suppl.),41,3 ad 6.
32. Ibid.,corp.; cp *Contra Gentiles* 3,126.
33. Ibid. ad 1.
34. ST III (Suppl.),41,4; Ibid. 49,5.
35. ST II-II,142,1.
36. E. C. Messenger, *Two in One Flesh: The Mystery of Sex in Marriage* (London: Sands,1948)2:178-179.
37. *Sententiae* 4,d.1,c.4.
38. Ibid., 4,d.2,c.1.
39. Ibid., d.26,c.6.

40. *Comment. in Libros Sententiarum* 4,d.26,a.14,q.2 ad 1.

41. *Comment in Quartum Librum Sent.* d.26,q.2,a.3; repeated in Suppl. 42,3c.

42. *Contra Gentiles* 4,78.

43. The details can be found in Mackin, *What is Marriage?* 145-175.

44. *Decretum* Pars II,Causa XXVII,Q.2,Cap.34,PL 187, 1406.

45. Code of Canon Law (1917),Can 1015,1; Code of Canon Law (1983), Can 1061,1.

46. *Catechism of the Council of Trent for Priests,* trans. J. Donovan (Rome: Propaganda Fidei, 1839), 641,643,661,653.

47. David E. Fellhauer, "The *Consortium Omnis Vitae* as a Juridical Element of Marriage," *Studia Canonica* 13:82.

48. Urban Navarrette, "Structura Juridica Matrimonii Secundum Concilium Vaticanum II," *Periodica* 56 (1967) 366.

49. Theodore Mackin, *What is Marriage?* (New York: Paulist, 1982) 214.

50. Gerald C. Treacy, ed., *Five Great Encyclicals* (New York: Paulist, 1939) 83-84.

51. Dietrich Von Hildebrand, *Marriage* (London: Longman's, 1939) v.

52. Ibid., 4 and vi.

53. Ibid., 6.

54. Ibid., 25. Emphasis in original.

55. Heribert Doms, *The Meaning of Marriage,* trans. George Sayer (London: Sheed and Ward, 1939) 94-95.

56. AAS 36 (1944) 103.

57. AAS 43 (1951) 848-849.

58. *Acta et Documenta Concilio Vaticano II Apparando.* Series II (*Praeparatoria*), Vol. 2, Pars 3 (Roma: Typis Polyglottis Vaticanis, 1968) 937.

59. Ibid., 910,n.16, and 917,note 50.

60. See Bernard Haring, *Commentary on the Documents of Vatican II* (New York: Herder,1969) 5:234.

61. *Church Dogmatics* (Edinburgh: Clark,1961), Vol. 3, Part 4,186.

5

The Sacrament of Marriage: Dissolution

The Scriptures of the Old Testament hold up to us the extreme fidelity of Hosea in his marriage despite every provocation from his faithless wife. They offer us also the exhortation of the later prophet Malachi to hate divorce, at least, as we saw ealier, divorce between Jew and Jew. That demand to be faithful and to hate divorce became the Christian gospel, a message and a challenge to all who claim to be followers of Jesus the Christ. The Gospels report four times that Jesus delivered a judgment against divorce and remarriage: in Matthew 5:32 and 19:9, in Luke 16:18, and in Mark 10:11-12. Paul, who writes well before any of the Gospel writers, also reports a prohibition of divorce and remarriage, and attributes it to the Lord (1 Cor 7:10-11). That message becomes the well-known, if not well-understood, law of the Catholic Church, namely that sacramental marriage is indissoluble. It is because both the gospel and the law that flows from it are not well-understood that reflection will be of help, not only to those Catholics who are married, but also to those countless others who have been married and are now separated or divorced or remarried, in understanding their marriage situation in the eyes of their Church.

In the public perception, perhaps even of Will and Willma as they approach marriage, the matter would appear to be simple and straightforward: the Roman Catholic Church does not allow divorce. But in Church theory and practice, the matter is far from that simple and straightforward. It appears useful, therefore, to cut through the confusion at the outset by setting out the long-established theory and practice of the Catholic Church, and then move toward its explanation and understanding. The 1983 *Code of Canon Law* states that theory and practice succinctly.

Canon 1141 states what kind of marriage cannot be dissolved by anyone. "A marriage which is ratified and consummated cannot be dissolved by any human power or by any cause other than death." There it is, almost as clear as crystal. The Catholic Church forbids divorce in the case of a ratified and consummated marriage. I say "almost as clear as crystal," for the canonical term *ratified* is not as clear as it needs to be; what it intends is more precise than what it actually says. It intends "a marriage which is ratified and consummated *as sacrament.*" There, now, is the teaching and the law of the Roman Catholic Church as clear as crystal. Only that marriage which is ratified and consummated as Christian sacrament is held to be indissoluble. Marriages between baptized persons which are not consummated are dissoluble, and are dissolved by the pope for just reason (Canon 1142). Marriages between nonbaptized persons, which are therefore nonsacramental, are dissoluble and are dissolved by the pope *in favorem fidei*, in favor of the faith (Canon 1143).

I hope it is already clear that the public understanding of the Catholic teaching and practice related to divorce and remarriage is simplistic, and needs to be refined. That the Roman Catholic Church forbids divorce is not entirely correct. That it forbids the dissolution by anyone, including the Roman Pontiff, of a marriage which is ratified and consummated as Christian sacrament, that is correct. That it forbids the dissolution by any merely human authority of any kind of valid marriage, that is correct; and therefore it does not accept as valid any dissolution of marriage by a civil court. But that it forbids the dissolution under every circumstance of any valid marriage, even by the bishop of Rome, that is quite incorrect. The rest of this chapter will be devoted to the explanation and understanding of these refinements.

Divorce and Remarriage in the New Testament

As noted, the Synoptic Gospels record words of Jesus about divorce and remarriage four times: in Mark 10:11-12, in Matthew 5:32 and 19:9, and in Luke 16:18. Paul reports a prohibition of divorce and remarriage, in 1 Corinthians 7:10-11, and attributes it to the Lord. To understand these New Testament passages to the fullest, we must first seek some understanding of the traditional Jewish understanding of divorce and remarriage within which they are embedded.

In Jesus' world marriage was a family affair in the specific sense that *families* married. "In the first-century Mediterranean world and earlier, marriage symbolizes the fusion of the honor of two extended families and is undertaken with a view to political and/or economic concerns."[1] Males draw up a marriage contract and eventually the father surrenders his daughter to the groom who takes her as his wife by bringing her into his own house. This process results in the disembedding of a daughter from the honor of her father and her embedding as wife in the honor of her new husband. It creates between husband and wife a bond that is not a legal bond, as it is in contemporary western society, but a sort of blood relationship called in shorthand a "one body" relationship. In the marriage a wife does not look to her husband for affection or companionship or comfort. She looks to him rather to be a good provider and an honorable citizen. Divorce was the reversal of this marriage process. "Divorce means the process of disembedding the female from the honor of the male, along with a sort of redistribution and return of the honor of the families concerned."[2] Divorce, like marriage, was a family affair.

The differences we need to note between both marriage and divorce in the time of Jesus and in our own time are clear. In modern western society, neither marriage nor divorce is a family affair in the sense just described. They are rather individual affairs. A man and a woman marry for love we say, seeking from one another interpersonal affection, companionship, support and comfort. They marry with or without the approval of their respective families. Their marriage creates between them not a blood bond, but a legal one. When they seek a divorce, therefore, they do not presume that they themselves can dissolve the marriage, but they petition the proper legal authority to do so. In the divorce proceedings, which either one may initiate, their concerns are never about extended family and honor, but about economics and property (and children). All of this reveals quite different presuppositions from those held in Jesus' day, not only among Jews but also among Romans. In Roman law, the spouses themselves dissolved their marriage, simply by withdrawing the consent which married them in the first place. Just as their free consent had married them, so also their free withdrawal of consent unmarried them. In Jewish law it was quite different. Only the husband could dissolve the marriage, and he did so simply by writing his wife a bill of divorce and dismissing her, a practice which was prescribed in Torah.

In the Book of Deuteronomy we read, "When a man takes a wife and marries her, if then she finds no favor in his eyes because he has found some indecency (*erwat dabar*) in her, and he writes her a bill of divorce and puts it in her hand and sends her out of his house, and she departs from his house, and if she goes and becomes another man's wife . . . then her former husband who sent her away may not take her again to be his wife, after she has been defiled" (24:1-4). This passage defines the right of the husband to divorce his wife, prohibits him from remarrying a spouse he has divorced and specifies the ground for divorce, *erwat dabar*, something indecent. This very general ground could only provoke dispute over its interpretation. In the generation prior to Jesus that dispute had created two camps, one following the Rabbi Hillel, the other following the Rabbi Shammai. Hillel and his disciples interpreted *erwat dabar* broadly. It intended serious moral, sexual delinquency, but also delinquency other than moral. Shammai and his school interpreted it strictly. It intended only serious, moral, sexual delinquency. The debate continued to rage at the time of Jesus, and it provides the context for Jesus' sayings about divorce in the Gospels.

Mark is the first of the Gospel writers, writing some thirty-five years after the death of Jesus. He writes, so tradition holds, for a Roman Christian community, a fact we shall have to bear in mind if we are to understand his passage correctly. That passage is in 10:2-12:

> Pharisees came up and in order to test him asked, "Is it lawful for a man to dismiss his wife?" He answered them, "What did Moses command you?" They said, "Moses permitted a man to write a certificate of divorce, and to dismiss her." But Jesus said to them, "For your hardness of heart he wrote you this commandment. But from the beginning of creation God made them male and female. For this reason a man shall leave his father and mother to be joined to his wife, and the two shall become one body. So they are no longer two but one body. What therefore God has joined together, let not man put asunder." And in the house the disciples asked him again about this matter. And he said to them, "Whoever dismisses his wife and marries another commits adultery against her. And if she dismisses her husband and marries another, she commits adultery."

The last sentence tells us first, the audience for which Mark was writing, and second, that the saying is probably not that of Jesus but an interpolation by Mark. That a wife would dismiss her husband is simply unheard of in the Palestinian Judaism of Jesus' day, and therefore it is improbable that Jesus said such a thing. It is, of course, a possibility in Roman law, and Mark has no qualms about interpreting the words of Jesus in light of the needs of his Roman Church. The author also presents the divorce tradition in the context of a dispute with the Pharisees. Now whether this context is from the historical life of Jesus, or from the life of Mark and his community, we have no way of knowing for sure. Ultimately, it does not matter, for in either case it is accepted as gospel by the Catholic Church.

The Pharisees set out, yet again (see also Mark 8:11 and 12:13), to test Jesus. This time they seek to test his honor and his allegiance in the dispute between Hillel and Shammai. Hence their question: "Is it lawful for a man to dismiss his wife?" Jesus replies with a question: "What did Moses command you?" Their reply refuses to acknowledge a command from

Moses, but only a permission. But Jesus insists on the nature of the Torah injunction as a command, given because of their unfaithfulness and hardness of heart. He insists that it was not so "from the beginning of creation," insinuating that Moses' commandment and their interpretation of it is an innovation which is counter to God's will be in the beginning. Pushing the discussion beyond Moses to the beginning brings into play everything that is in the Genesis story about male and female; bone of bone and flesh of flesh; a man leaving his father and his mother to cleave to his wife, to become with her one body.

Jesus' argument against the Pharisees is that God's will from the beginning was that a man and a woman are so joined in marriage that before God, and therefore before the people, they are one person. How, then, could a man dismiss this one person, his very own person in divorce? We saw earlier the same argument made by the author of the letter to the Ephesians: "Husbands should love their wives as their own bodies; he who loves his wife loves himself" (5:28). Jesus' conclusion, and his teaching as articulated by Mark, is that marriage is intended by God from the beginning to be indissoluble. "What therefore God has joined together, let not man put asunder," not even a Jewish man claiming to follow Torah. In the literarily contrived conversation "in the house," Mark articulates in a parable saying what it all means for the disciples of Jesus, in Jesus' day, in Mark's day and in our day. "Whoever divorces his wife and marries another commits adultery against her." For the sake of his Roman audience, Mark extends that to the case, theoretically impossible in Jewish law, but perfectly possible in Roman law, of the wife dismissing her husband.

Matthew has two versions of Jesus's sayings on divorce, a short one and a long one. The short one is located within the Sermon on the Mount. "It was also said, 'Whoever divorces his wife, let him give her a certificate of divorce.' But I say to you that everyone who divorces his wife, except on the ground of *porneia*, makes her an adulteress; and whoever marries a divorced woman commits adultery" (5:31-32). The long one is situated in the context of a dispute between Jesus and the Pharisees, who seek to test him. In outline it is very similar to Mark's version, probably because Matthew borrowed it from Mark, but there are significant differences of detail.

The test to which Jesus is submitted in Matthew is again a test of whether he sides with Hillel or Shammai in the debate about *erwat dabar,* or *porneia*, as the Septuagint version translates it. The Pharisees ask him: "Is it lawful to divorce one's wife for any cause?" (19:3). A positive answer would have placed Jesus on the side of Hillel's broad interpretation; a negative answer would have placed him on the side of Shammai's restrictive one. We can surmise that the test was designed to test Jesus' honor and to cause him to lose the adherents of either Hillel or Shammai. But, as in Mark, though this time more quickly, Jesus refuses the terms of the question, and returns the discussion to "the beginning" (19:4) chronicled in Genesis, in which it "was not so" (19:8).

Jesus' teaching is the same as in Mark. "They are no longer two but one body. What therefore God has joined together, let not man put asunder" (19:6). Also as in Mark, though with a significant addition, there is the ultimate conclusion. "Whoever divorces his wife, except for *porneia*, and marries another, commits adultery. And he who marries a divorced woman commits adultery" (19:9). Jesus' response to the test is to refuse to side with either Hillel or Shammai and to return the discussion to a question more radical than the one about legitimate cause for divorce. He seeks to have them ask whether divorce is humanly possible at all, and answers negatively, because such is what God, an authority greater than Moses, intended in the beginning.

Jesus' position and his teaching about divorce and remarriage would have been indisputably clear were it not for that exceptive phrase, except for *porneia*, found in both of Matthew's versions but not in Mark's or Luke's. The meaning of that phrase, as can be expected, has been as endlessly disputed as the meaning of *erwat dabar*. I shall not enter that dispute in this book, since I am persuaded that we cannot now know beyond debate the meaning of the phrase in Matthew's intent.[3]

I wish to raise here a different question: does the exceptive clause originate in the teaching of Jesus or in the authorship of Matthew? Is it from that stratum of the gospel which faithfully records the words and deeds of Jesus, or is it from that stratum which derives from the author in the light of the needs of his Christian community? I accept the majority scholarly opinion that the latter is the case, given Matthew's acknowledged penchant for adding to the words of Jesus for his own purposes, and given the absence of the phrase in Mark, Luke, and Paul. I wish to underscore only one conclusion from that. Being fully aware of Jesus' position on divorce and remarriage, Matthew did not hesitate to make an addition to it in the light of the needs of his Church. That Church, all are agreed, was a Jewish-Christian Church, that is, one composed of Jews who had been "converted" to Christianity, but who still adhered to the Jewish law.

Paul, too, did not hesitate to contribute his own interpretation. In chapter seven of his First Letter to the Corinthians, written long before any of the Gospels, perhaps as early as the year 52, Paul provides answers to questions posed to him by the Corinthian community. That community was a mixed Jewish-Gentile community, which explains Paul's choice of words for his instruction on divorce. Sometimes he has Jewish law in mind, in which only the husband has the power to dismiss the wife; sometimes he has the Roman law in mind, in which both husband and wife have the power to dismiss the other. In apparent response to a question about divorce Paul offers a command, which he claims is from the Lord. "To the married I give charge, not I but the Lord, that a wife is not to be separated from her husband. And if she is separated, she is to remain unmarried or is to be reconciled to her husband. And a husband is not to dismiss his wife" (7:10-11).

The custom of divorce was deeply rooted in the traditions that the Corinthians knew, and it is not difficult to imagine them wishing to know what they were supposed to do about it as Christians. Paul leaves them in no doubt what should be their attitude as Christians: "the wife is not to be separated from her husband," nor is the husband to dismiss his wife. It would appear, from the verbs he uses, that Paul has in mind the divorce custom common to both Jewish and Roman law, that is, the dismissal of the wife by the husband. The husband is not to dismiss his wife, and the wife is not to be separated (that is, by someone else) from her husband.

Having dealt with the question of divorce in the case of the marriage of two Christians, Paul then proceeds to the discussion of a case of conscience about divorce that must have been prevalent in the earliest Christian communities, as it is still prevalent in mission communities today. The case is this: what about divorce in the marriage in which one spouse has become Christian and the other has remained nonChristian? Paul has two pieces of advice for the spouses in such marriages, each of them hinging on the attitude of the nonChristian spouse.

The first advice covers the case in which the nonChristian partner is willing to continue to live with the Christian spouse. In this case, "if any brother has a wife who is an unbeliever, and she consents to live with him, he should not dismiss her. If any woman has a husband who is an unbeliever, and he consents to live with her, she should not dismiss him" (7:12-13). It would appear that Paul is now thinking firmly within the context of Roman law, in which both husband and wife have the right to end the marriage by dismissing the other. And his instruction is firm: when the unbelieving spouse is willing to live in marriage with the believer, he or she is not to be dismissed. The Genesis instruction stands firm: what God has joined together, let not man put asunder.

As it did in the time of Ezra and Nehemiah and Malachi, however, that teaching comes under interpretation and exception in Paul's second bit of advice. What of the case in which the unbeliever is unwilling to continue to live in marriage with the believer? "But if the unbelieving spouse desires to separate in such matters . . ." (7:15). Notice the verb. It is separate, a verb which indicates an action which the agent does. It is the unbeliever who separates himself or herself; he is not separated, or dismissed, by the believing spouse. There is no suggestion that the marriage of the believer and the unbeliever is not a valid marriage. There is no suggestion that Jesus' remembered instruction does not apply to it. There is only the suggestion that in this case Paul is making an exception (*"I* say, not the Lord," 7:12). And the sole reason he gives for the exception is "the brother or sister is not to play the slave in such matters. For God has called us to peace" (7:15). It is an interesting reason, both then and now.

In this second scenario, the attempt of the Christian spouse to hold the nonChristian spouse to the marriage, the attempt to bring him or her back to the marriage, to seek the reconciliation Paul had already recommended for Christian spouses (7:11), would simply destroy the peace to which a Christian is called by God. It is, as we have said, an interesting reason for an exception to Jesus' well remembered instruction, in America today as in Corinth in the past. Peace, it seems, is a greater value than preserving a valid marriage. The Roman Catholic Church sanctioned this reason and this approach to dissolving a valid marriage in the twelfth century, still sanctions them today, and names the process the Pauline Privilege.

We are now in a position to reflect on the New Testament teaching on divorce and remarriage. Our first reflection must be that it is not at all correct to speak of the New Testament *teaching*, for there are several *teachings*, and they are not in agreement. Nor are they all derived solely from Jesus, as is frequently and simplisticly claimed and advanced as the reason why the Roman Catholic must continue to oppose divorce and remarriage.

There is a well remembered saying of Jesus which scholars agree is probably original as reported in Luke 16:18: "Everyone who divorces his wife and marries another commits adultery." In Luke's redaction the saying is an isolated one. But in both Mark and Matthew it is located in a careful literary setting to highlight not only its importance but also its difficulty. Mark (10:2-12) offers the saying at the conclusion of a "discussion" with the Pharisees, though Jesus does not make the statement before the Pharisees but before his disciples when he is alone with them later. "Now such a setting for a saying is quite familiar in Mark. It is the ordinary trapping of mystery (cf. Mark 6:10,37; 7:17; 9:33 etc)."[4]

Matthew (19:3-12) also presents the saying in the context of a dispute with the Pharisees. He, however, has Jesus state it in the public disputation and then explain it later to the disciples. This is his standard way of presenting particularly difficult material. The explanation of the saying is the parable of the eunuchs: ". . . there are eunuchs who have been so from birth, and there are eunuchs who have been made so by men, and there are eunuchs who have made themselves eunuchs for the sake of the kingdom of heaven'' (19:12). What clarification does the eunuch parable bring to Jesus' traditional saying about divorce? Only that it is a saying not about divorce at all but about remarriage after divorce.

The prevailing Jewish tradition about a marriage in which there was *erwat dabar* or *porneia* was that a husband had to divorce his wife and could not remarry her, though he could marry someone else. The eunuch parable clarifies Jesus' saying about divorce by explaining that, though a husband could divorce his wife if there was *porneia*, he could not remarry either her or anyone else. Matthew knows this is a hard saying. That is the very point of the objection made by the disciples: "If such is the case of a man with his wife, it is not expedient to marry" (19:10). Many of the sayings of Jesus that Matthew reports are hard, sayings about plucking out your eye (5:29), about cutting off your hand (5:30), about selling your goods and giving the proceeds to the poor (8:21), about losing your life to find it (10:39), about taking up your cross (16:24). But neither Jesus nor Matthew retreats from the saying. Rather he reinforces it, explaining that it is not a demand made of everyone but only of those who would be his disciples. "He who is able to receive this," therefore, "let him receive it" (19:12).

Jesus is reported as saying: "Every one who divorces his wife and marries another commits adultery." Malina argues that "if this is what Jesus said, it has to be a parable." For "when taken literally, it makes as little sense as 'you are the salt of the earth' or 'you are the light of the world,' " and "in the Gospels of Matthew and Mark this teaching requires further, private explanation, a procedure these authors use for parables."[5] If it is a parable, it requires further interpretation for the concrete circumstances in which its hearers find themselves. That concrete interpretation is exactly what the New Testament writers provide.

Mark adds something that Jesus could never have said in his context, for it would have made no sense to say it to a Jewish audience. That addition prohibits a wife from dismissing her husband (Mark 10:12). Matthew, good Jew that he is, adds his exceptive clause—except for *erwat dabar* or *porneia*—whatever it meant in his mind. Paul adds his own genuine exception, covering the case of a marriage in which an unbelieving spouse wishes no longer to live with a believing one. Whatever personal preference anyone might have, I believe Mackin's judgment cannot be gainsayed. "Because every element of the instruction on divorce and remarriage is part of the Gospel (and this includes the instruction in 1 Corinthians, even that part coming from Paul himself), it would falsify our reading of this Gospel if we were to single out one element, play it off against the others and make it override them."[6] Such a ploy would, indeed, falsify the New Testament Tradition so sacred to Christians.

Diverging accounts of the question of divorce and remarriage, as of many other important things, are an integral part of the New Testament tradition, as the disciples of Jesus sought to bring the meaning of his life and death and resurrection into their lives. There are diverging accounts, we now believe, because divergent Christian communities had divergent pressing concerns that needed to be answered. That is what Mark did, and Matthew and Paul. That the popular wisdom in the later Catholic tradition singled out one element in those diverging accounts, namely, the element of the indissolubility of a marriage, and allowed that element to override all the others, ought never be allowed to obscure the original divergence.

We can conclude this section by reflecting on an important teaching of the Second Vatican Council, for we are now in a position to grasp its full import. "The sacred authors wrote the four gospels, selecting some things from the many which had been handed on by word of mouth or in writing, reducing some of them to a synthesis, explicating some things in view of the situation of their churches, and preserving the form of proclamation, but always in such fashion that *they told the honest truth about Jesus*" (DV 19). So did the sacred authors in the instructions on divorce and remarriage.

The authors selected, reduced, added and still told us the honest truth about Jesus. That honest truth would appear to be that Jesus taught that the one-body marriage, willed by God from the beginning, constitutes a man and a woman in such an interpersonal communion that every human authority is forbidden to dissolve it. Note *forbidden* to dissolve it, and not *powerless* to dissolve it, because probably Matthew and certainly Paul did not believe that is what Jesus intended. Believing this, they formulated their own version of the aphorism: What God has joined together let not man put asunder—except in the case of . . . . The Roman Catholic Church, as we shall now see, has followed that formulation for centuries and continues to follow it today.

The Development of the New Testament Teaching in the Church

In the first three centuries of the existence of the Christian church, Jesus' saying about divorce and remarriage was reinforced. Included in the understanding of Jesus' teaching was the exceptive clause in Matthew, which was taken to be the word of Jesus himself. But there were uncertainties about interpretation, both in theory and in practice. In a book composed, as the Muratorian canon says, "in the city of Rome, by Hermas, while his brother Pius was sitting on the throne of the church of the city of

Rome," between the years 140 and 154, we learn something of interest. The book *The Shepherd of Hermas* is divided into a series of visions, mandates, and parables. In Mandate IV we find a conversation between Hermas and his shepherd, the Angel of Penitence, relating to the question of divorce and remarriage.

Hermas asks, "If a man has a wife who believes in the Lord and he surprises her in adultery, does he commit a sin if he lives with her?" The angel's reply is two-pronged. If a man does not know of his wife's sin, then he does not sin in living with her. "But, if her husband knows the sin, and she does not repent but persists in her fornication, he becomes guilty of her sin as long as he lives with her." Hermas asks then, what is a husband to do in this latter case? "Let him dismiss her and remain single. But if he dismisses her and marries another woman, he himself commits adultery." The adulterous wife must be dismissed for adultery, but the husband must remain unmarried "to bring about her repentance."[7] This teaching provides a good summary of the marriage ethic of an early Christian Church. A spouse, at least a wife, must be dismissed for unrepentant adultery. Such dismissal, though, in contrast to the established practice of Roman law, does not constitute a dissolution of the marriage, but merely a separation. Neither spouse, therefore, is free to remarry.

The fourth century was a time of great development in doctrine and discipline in both the eastern and the western Christian Churches, including doctrine and discipline with respect to divorce and remarriage. In the east, two great bishops, Basil of Caesarea and John Chrysostom of Constantinople, lastingly shaped the marriage doctrine and discipline of the eastern Churches. Two great Fathers, Jerome and especially Augustine, did the same for the Latin Church. We must, therefore, consider the teachings of these men.

Basil deals with separation and remarriage in Rule 73 of his *Moralia*. Appealing predictably to Matthew 5:31-32, he prescribes that "a husband should not separate from his wife, nor a wife from her husband, unless the other spouse be taken in adultery or be an obstacle to piety." Matthew's exceptive clause, taken at the time to be a saying of the Lord's, is accepted without demur as a legitimate cause for separation. Indeed, throughout the East, the adultery of one spouse imposed upon the other the obligation to separate from him or her. But after such separation could either spouse remarry? In his *Moralia*, Basil replies no. "It is not permitted to a husband who has dismissed his wife to marry another. Nor is it permitted to a wife who has been repudiated by her husband to marry another."[8]

Basil's rule concerns only the case of the husband who has dismissed his wife and the wife who has been dismissed. But what of the case where one spouse abandons the other? What may the abandoned spouse do? Basil responds to that question as put to him by another bishop, Amphilocius. First, he points out, the Lord's word applies equally to husbands and wives: they are both forbidden to abandon marriage except for adultery. The case in which one spouse abandons the other is resolved on the basis of whether one is the abandoner or the abandoned. "The woman who leaves her husband is an adulteress if she goes to another husband. But the husband who is abandoned is worthy of pardon, and a woman who lives with him is not condemned. But if a husband who has dismissed his wife goes to another, he is an adulterer because he makes her commit adultery. And the woman who lives with him is an adulterer, because she has drawn to herself another's husband."[9]

Recognizing a gospel demand deriving from Jesus, Basil's Church still showed compassion for innocent spouses who had been abandoned. That compassion created a reluctance to charge them with adultery if they remarried. That charge was reserved for a spouse who dismissed his or her partner and remarried, for a man who married a woman who had been dismissed by her husband, for a woman who married a man who had dismissed his wife unjustly, and also for a woman who dismissed her husband even justly and then remarried. Basil later reports the compassionate treatment of a husband who had abandoned his wife and remarried. The man had done "penance with tears" and, after seven years, he was accepted back "among the faithful."[10] Here Basil sets out the conditions in his Church for the return to full communion among the faithful of the man who has abandoned his wife. The second marriage seems to be accepted and the sending away of the second wife or the taking back of the first are not listed among the conditions for full communion.

John Chrysostom is regarded as the most influential teacher in the eastern Church. His teaching about divorce and remarriage is as confused as that of all his contemporaries. On the one hand, he warns wives that they must not leave their husbands, even if their marriage is intolerable. On the other hand, arguing that Paul has given wives a permission to leave, he allows that they may leave and need not be obligated to return to their husbands. He forbids them, however, to remarry. In his homily on First Corinthians 7, he first sets forth the classic Judaeo-Christian ethic of the time, that is, in the case of adultery spouses *must* separate, and then he goes further, arguing that the adultery of the wife dissolves a marriage, leaving the husband no longer a husband.

Chrysostom uses the legal divorce word *dialuein*, which raises some interesting questions. Does Chrysostom believe that the adultery of the wife, which is what he speaks of in his homily, or the adultery of the husband, which he does not speak of, dissolve their marriage in the very same way as a legal divorce? Can both then remarry, or at least the one not guilty of *porneia*? He does not say, and so we can only guess. What we can say with certainty is that the opinions of Basil and Chrysostom shaped the present practice of the eastern Churches, which is that an *innocent* spouse in any divorce proceeding may be remarried in a church ceremony and incur no ecclesiastical penalty. The doctrine and discipline in the western or Roman Catholic Church is quite different. There, as we have seen, a marriage which is both a Christian sacrament and consummated cannot be dissolved by any human authority. Consequently, any attempt at divorce is null and, therefore, any attempt at remarriage after divorce is null. We must now examine the source of that doctrine and discipline in two great Western Fathers, Jerome and, especially, Augustine.

In his commentary on Matthew's gospel, Jerome deals with the exceptive clause. He explains that a wife's fornication (his translation of *porneia*) has put an end to the marital affection that exists in a marriage, and has rent the one-body union in two. The adulterous wife has separated herself from her husband, and he must separate from her lest he be condemned also. He quotes Proverbs 18:22; " 'Whoever keeps an adulterous wife is stupid and impious.' Wherever, therefore, there is fornication, and suspicion of fornication, a wife may be freely dismissed."[11] But what then? May the husband who has dismissed his wife because of adultery remarry? Jerome replies no, for the following reason. "It could happen that a man may falsely accuse an innocent wife, and because he wants a second marriage impute crime to the first. Therefore he is commanded not to dismiss his first wife so that he may take a second one while she lives."[12]

Jerome's meaning here is both clear and unclear. It is clear to the extent that he judges that a husband who has legitimately dismissed his wife may not remarry. It is unclear, however, why he may not remarry. Is he forbidden to remarry only to protect a possibly falsely accused wife? If it were demonstrated that the wife were guilty of adultery, could he then remarry? Jerome provides an answer in an earlier letter to his friend Amandus. Amandus had posed several questions to him, among them one that asked if a woman who had left her husband on the grounds of adultery and had been forced into a second marriage could participate in the life of the Church. Jerome's answer is short and unmistakably clear: "If a woman gives herself to another man while her husband is alive, she is an adulteress."[13] He claims this response is derived from Paul's words in Romans 7:1 and 1 Corinthians 7:39. And so there passed into Western Christian history an interpretation of the New Testament message: yes, indeed, a spouse may be dismissed for *porneia,* but such dismissal does not dissolve the marriage and enable either spouse to remarry another.

It is but a separation, a separation from bed and board as the medievals would later say, claiming Jerome as their justification.

Much more powerfully influential than Jerome on the marriage-divorce doctrine and discipline of the Roman Church was Augustine, Bishop of Hippo, whom we met in the preceding chapter. His teaching is found most directly and systematically in *On Adulterous Marriages*, a book he wrote in 419 to refute Pelagian errors. Bishop Pollentius had his own interpretation of the New Testament data on divorce and remarriage. A husband and wife who are not guilty of adultery have these options: they may remain married or they may separate on the initiative of one of them who finds the marriage insupportable or who wishes to live a celibate life. If they do separate, and the one finds a celibate life impossible, they may not remarry any other, but must return to one another. A husband or a wife whose spouse had committed adultery may divorce the spouse and remarry. In his reply Augustine deals with each of these points in turn.

There is no question at all in a nonadulterous marriage. Where no adultery is involved, neither spouse may leave the marriage and certainly may not marry another. Only one reason justifies a spouse to abandon a marriage or to dismiss the other spouse: the other's adultery. When one spouse has left the other because of the other's adultery, even the innocent spouse may not remarry, exactly as Paul said. "We say that, when both spouses are Christian, it is not permitted to a woman who has left her husband because of fornication to marry another, and it is not permitted to a woman under any circumstances to leave her husband who has not committed fornication."[14] Augustine, as did Jerome, apparently understood that the dismissal of a spouse for adultery, warranted by both Matthew's exceptive clause and the accepted ethic of the early Church, did not effect a true dissolution of the marriage but only a separation. So the western tradition has understood him to mean.

This was not the first time Augustine had confronted the questions of divorce and remarriage. He had already dealt with them in his commentary on the Sermon on the Mount, where we find some points of interest for us. He accepts the exceptive clause as coming from the Lord and insists on what we have already heard him saying. It is not permitted to dismiss a wife except on the ground of fornication, which is his translation of Matthew's *porneia*. In the case of fornication, a wife does not have to be dismissed but may be dismissed, but neither she nor her husband may then marry another.

There remains always the question of remarriage after dismissal. We have already heard him say that a wife must remain unmarried as long as her husband lives, and a husband must remain unmarried as long as his wife lives. But there is a case about which he professes to be doubtful.

"If a wife is dismissed by her husband, with whom she wishes to remain, whoever marries her commits adultery, but whether she is guilty of the same crime is uncertain."[15] He does admit that it is hard to see how one spouse can be guilty of adultery and the other not, but the point of great interest here is that Augustine, not much given to hedged statements, does profess uncertainty. If he really believed unequivocally that dismissal of a spouse in every circumstance merely achieved a separation of the spouses, and not a dissolution of the marriage, would he have had such uncertainty?

Earlier in *The Good of Marriage*, directed against the Manichees, Augustine had no uncertainty. He asks whether, since the Scriptures permit a husband to dismiss his wife for adultery, the husband may remarry. He replies, first that the Scriptures themselves make a "difficult knot" out of the question. Then, secondly, he gives a quite unequivocal answer. "I do not see how a man can have the freedom to marry another after dismissing an adulterous wife, since a woman does not have the freedom to marry another after dismissing an adulterous husband." So indissolubly strong is the bond between a married couple that "though it is entered into for the purpose of procreation, it is not loosed for the purpose of procreation."[16] Spouses in an infertile marriage may not, therefore, divorce and remarry another in order to procreate children.

Augustine ultimately justifies his teaching by drawing the whole question of marriage and divorce into his theology of the *sacramentum*. "I do not think it (the marriage bond) could have such strength unless it were some kind of *sacramentum* of something greater than would arise from our weak mortality, something that remains unshaken even in the face of men who desert this bond and attempt to dissolve it. The marriage bond is not dissolved by divorce so that, even though separated, the spouses remain married to one another, and both husband and wife commit adultery with those to whom they are married after divorce." At the end of it all, he adds a crucial explanatory statement: "but only in the City of God (Augustine's well-known figure for the Church), on his holy mountain, is such the case with a wife."[17]

Several things are now clear about Augustine's teaching. First, the marriage bond is such that even divorce does not dissolve it, not even divorce from a spouse guilty of fornication/adultery. Divorce, dismissal, abandonment achieves only a separation of the spouses, leaving them still married. Second, the resistance of the marriage bond to any effort to dissolve it is due to the fact that it is a *sacramentum* of something else. Third, this *sacramentum* is found only within the City of God, the Christian Church; only marriages between Christians, therefore, are indissoluble. All that is clear.

One question remains. Of what is the marriage bond a *sacramentum* or symbol? Augustine is quite clear about the answer. "Just as the *sacramentum* of plural marriages in times gone by signified the future multitude of peoples on earth subject to God, so in our day the *sacramentum* of the monogamous marriage signifies the future unity of all of us subject to God in one heavenly city."[18] Marriage in the City of God, that is, marriage between Christians, is a sacrament or symbol for Augustine. But we need to be careful here. It is a sacrament, not of the present union of God and his people or of Christ and his Church, as we have frequently described it throughout this work, but of the future unity between God and his people in the heavenly city. Only later, in his *On Marriage and Concupiscence*, he will draw formally on the language of the Letter to the Ephesians to speak of Christian marriage as a sacrament of the unity between Christ and the Church.

Both Jerome's and Augustine's marriage doctrine and discipline were bequeathed to the Roman Church and, because of their accumulated prestige, controlled its developing theology and discipline of marriage. Augustine's theology in particular, especially his theology of the sacrament, however inchoately worked out, became of enduring significance. Its influence on the present marriage doctrine and discipline of the Catholic Church is hard to overestimate.

We have already met Gratian, that great collector of opinions, and his distinction between initiated and completed marriage. That distinction became the basis of his teaching on the indissolubility and dissolubility of marriage. An initiated marriage, not yet consummated by sexual intercourse, can be dissolved and the former spouses are quite free to remarry others. A marriage completed by sexual intercourse is quite indissoluble, so that if the spouses divorce, even if for the legitimate cause of adultery, the bond of their marriage remains and neither is free to remarry. His judgment on the question of indissolubility is beyond doubt. "Everything which has been adduced concerning the nondissolution of marriage is understood of a completed marriage, one initiated by espousal and consummated by the duty of sexual intercourse. What has been said about a dissoluble marriage, on the other hand, is understood of an initiated marriage, one which has not yet been consummated by the fulfillment of that duty."[19] With this judgment, Gratian helped establish in the Roman Church the tradition that a marriage not yet consummated by sexual intercourse may be dissolved.

Some twenty years after the compilation of Gratian's *Decree* at Bologna, a theologian at Paris made yet another compilation, this time of theological opinions. He was called Peter Lombard and his compilation was called *Sententiae*, that is, opinions, of Fathers, councils, popes, and theologians who preceded him. Despite the fact that it is largely unoriginal, the *Sententiae* became an enormously important work in medieval theology, one that subsequent theologians had to cite obligatorily. The sole thing that concerns us here, though, is what Lombard contributed to the Catholic tradition of marriage and divorce. That contribution lies in his expansion of Augustine's notion of sacrament.

Lombard accepts Augustine's three goods of marriage: faith, offspring, sacrament. It is what he says of sacrament that is of interest to us here, for he extends the meaning of it beyond what Augustine intended. "Note," he teaches, "that the third good of marriage is called *sacramentum*, not in the sense that it is the marriage itself, but because the marriage is a sign of that sacred reality which is the spiritual and inseparable union of Christ and the church.''[20] For Augustine *sacramentum* was the commitment of the spouses to one another never to separate. For Lombard, it is a characteristic of the marriage, a characteristic that makes it an image of the union of Christ and the Church.

A marriage between Christians, Lombard argues, can exist without the fidelity of the spouses; it can exist without offspring. But it cannot exist without the *sacramentum*, reflecting the union between Christ and the Church. Since it is this sacrament that makes a marriage indissoluble, it is a small step to the conclusion that where there is no sacrament a marriage can be dissolved. With this conclusion, all the elements for the present Roman Catholic approach to the question of dissolubility-indissolubility are now historically in place. Gratian contributes the teaching that only a consummated marriage is indissoluble. Lombard contributes that only a sacramental marriage reflecting the union between Christ and the Church is indissoluble. From these two positions will grow the modern Roman Catholic teaching: only the consummated, sacramental marriage is beyond every power to dissolve. But before considering that teaching as it appears in the *Code of Canon Law*, we must consider one more relevant medieval development in the area of marriage dissolubility.

The nonconsummated marriage was, in fact, not the only one Gratian judged to be dissoluble. He outlines this case. A married pagan is converted to the Christian faith and, out of hatred for the faith, his wife leaves him. He then takes a Christian woman as his wife. Gratian poses several questions, only two of which touch us here. The first question is this: can there be a valid marriage among pagans? The second is: may the man take a second wife while his first wife lives? His answer to the first question is a straightforward yes, there is true and valid marriage among pagans. His answer to the second question employs a distinction we will recognize from Paul. If the wife wishes to remain in the marriage, she should not be dismissed against her will; if she is dismissed, the husband may not remarry. If the wife does not wish to remain in the marriage, she may be permitted to leave and the husband is free to marry another. This regulation, he insists, applies only to those married while pagans, never to those married while Christians.

Several points of importance to our discussion of Roman Catholic marriage theory and practice may now be underscored. First, there is valid marriage among pagans, but it is not indissoluble marriage since it is not sacramental. Second, a valid pagan marriage may be dissolved when one of the spouses becomes a Christian, but only if the pagan spouse remains a pagan and leaves the marriage. Third, if the pagan spouse refuses to live with the now-Christian partner and departs, the Christian is free to remarry according to Church law. After Gratian, several popes will extend the scope of this procedure, now called the Pauline Privilege, and a brief consideration of their rulings will bring us up to the present practice.

In the sixteenth century circumstances in missionary Africa and the Indies forced upon Rome decisions extending the Pauline Privilege. The first of these decisions was made by Paul III in 1537. The decision looked to the case of pagan husbands in the Indies who were in polygamous marriages and who sought baptism. It prescribed that if the husband seeking to become a Christian could remember which of his wives he had married first, he was to keep her and dismiss all the others. But if he could not remember which wife he had married first, he could keep whichever wife he chose and dismiss all the others. In this latter case, the pope would dissolve the marriage between him and his "forgotten" first wife, so that both could then remarry without penalty. Though this was treated at the time as an extension of the Pauline Privilege, we can note that it was much more than a simple extension. For the one characteristic which had consistently characterized the Pauline Privilege, from Paul's first articulation of it right up to the time of Paul III, that remarriage is permissible only in the case in which the pagan spouse departs, and not at all in the case in which she is dismissed, is now ignored. A husband is granted the privilege of retaining whichever wife he wishes and of dismissing all others.

In 1561 Pius V made yet another ruling in this case. He ruled that a converted polygamous husband could retain as his wife that one of his wives who was willing to receive baptism along with him. He ruled thus, moreover, as he explicitly states, on his own will and initiative, not on the basis of any biblical or theological or canonical tradition. Pius' ruling, claiming as it did that he had the power to specify which would be the legitimate wife of a converted polygamous husband and to dissolve all other marriages, including that of an unconverted first wife, was an enormous departure from established Church law and practice. So enormous was it that canonists of the time urged that it be applied only in the case in which the genuinely first (and, therefore, presumedly legitimate) wife could not be found or identified. Such a procedure, they argued, would at least ensure that known consummated marriages would not be dissolved.

A final ruling touching our question was delivered in 1585 by Gregory XIII. Gregory's ruling looked to another problem, namely, the problem created when a husband or a wife is carried off into slavery and thereby separated from his or her spouse. What should happen if the now separated spouse sought baptism and wished to marry again? The established procedure of the Pauline Privilege was to inquire from the pagan spouse whether he or she would live at peace with the newly converted Christian. In the case of the separation caused by enslavement, such an inquiry was not possible. Gregory granted a dispensation from the inquiry in such cases and exercised his claimed papal power to dissolve the previous pagan marriage.

All these rulings were considered at the time of their publication as extensions of the Pauline Privilege. But they go so far beyond the Pauline terms of that privilege that whether they are extensions of it, or whether they are quite new privileges introduced by the papal power to bind and loose, was and still is hotly disputed. Those who consider them an exercise of the power to bind and loose, and not an extension of the biblically warranted Pauline Privilege, name them the "Petrine Privilege." Whatever one chooses to call them, however, such rulings and practices clarify one thing. They make clear that the Catholic claim that marriage is indissoluble is not to be understood as broadly as it appears on the surface. Rather it is to be interpreted as narrowly as it has been in both the theory and the practice of the Catholic Church. Only those marriages which are both sacramental and consummated are indissoluble.

Divorce and Remarriage in the Catholic Church: Present Practice

Recently, I dealt with this case. Two people who had been married twenty-eight years decided to separate. On talking to the husband, who is quite a religious man, I discovered that one of the great pains he was suffering was that he felt he could no longer participate in the sacramental life of the Church. The Catholic Church, he believed, does not allow married people to separate. I was able to explain to him that he was quite wrong. Being separated or being divorced does not cut off a Catholic from participation in the full life of the Church. Indeed, recognizing the pain and distress that separation or divorce often produces, the Church urges those who are in either situation to participate as fully as possible in sacramental life as a means of personal support. However much the failure of a marriage may be interpreted as a failure to live up to the Gospel, and whether it is or is not such a failure is to be decided only in each individual case, there is no canonical penalty for getting either a civil separation or a civil divorce. Civilly divorced Catholics incur canonical penalties only when they remarry while their previous spouse is still alive.

Notice, in the previous sentence, that I was careful to specify *civil* divorce. For, though the Catholic Church's reading of the Gospel leads it to look upon all valid marriages as indissoluble, it does dissolve valid marriages. In straight English, it does grant divorces, under certain conditions, as we have seen. The most ancient of those "divorce" processes is the one known as the Pauline Privilege, which we have already sufficiently explained. Two unbaptized persons are married; one of them now wishes to be baptized into the Catholic Church and the other refuses to live with him or her in peace; if the unbaptized spouse departs from the marriage, the church considers it dissolved and will issue a declaration to that effect, leaving both parties free to remarry. As we have seen, the Pauline Privilege has either been extended into, or has been augmented by, the Petrine Privilege on the basis of the assumed authority of the pope to bind and loose, even to loose valid marriages.

There is yet another way to dissolve a valid marriage in the Catholic Church. The ancient Roman answer to the question of when did a marriage actually take place was that it took place when the marrying couple freely consented to be married. The ancient northern European answer was that it took place when the couple engaged in their first sexual intercourse after the giving of that consent. The medieval Church combined these two opinions and taught that a marriage was initiated by consent and consummated or completed by sexual intercourse. If, after the giving of consent, which initiates a valid marriage, there has been no sexual intercourse, then the marriage may be dissolved, leaving both parties free to remarry without any Church penalty.

Besides these ways to dissolve a marriage in the Catholic Church, there is that other now-famous, or perhaps infamous, process known as "annulment." It is quite a different process from the dissolution processes already considered, for while those processes dissolve a marriage believed to be valid, annulment is a judgment that there never was at any time a valid marriage between these two people. It is common knowledge that today ecclesiastical annulments are granted more frequently than ever before. In 1969, about seven hundred annulments were granted in the United States; in 1985, the last year for which I have statistics, that number had risen fiftyfold to 36,180. Thanks to new procedural norms and to the broadening of grounds for annulment, some church lawyers argue today that virtually every failed marriage that comes before a Church tribunal can be annulled. That feeling has become so pervasive that it has also become a source of controversy within the Church, some arguing that granting an annulment has become too easy, others arguing that it should be liberalized even further to respond to the needs of hurting people. The London *Tablet* reported in 1987 that, in a speech to the Roman Rota, Pope John Paul II deplored "the excessive proliferation and almost automatic annulment of marriages on pretexts of immaturity and diminished responsibilty."[21]

Grounds for annulment are multiple: lack of the proper canonical form, that is, the requirement for Catholics to wed in the presence of a designated priest and two witnesses; lack of intention to have children; somehow defective consent, as a result, for instance, of grave fear or force or ignorance; prior intention to be unfaithful; prior mental illness or alcoholism or psychosexual problems; general immaturity at the time of the marriage. It has been calculated that immaturity, variously called lack of due discretion, psychic incapacity, psychic irregularity, moral impotency, is involved in about 90 percent of the annulment cases that come before tribunals, leading some canon lawyers to suggest that virtually every failed marriage can be annulled on that basis.

Summary

This chapter has been about the theory and the practice of marriage, divorce and remarriage in the Roman Catholic tradition. It is summarized in two major ideas and a minor one. The first major idea is that the popular wisdom about divorce and remarriage in the Catholic tradition is simplistic and wide of the mark. The position of the Church, easily discerned from its long-standing practice, is abundantly clear. Only that marriage which is consummated as Christian sacrament is indissoluble; every other type of marriage not only is dissoluble but also has been dissolved by the Church at one time or another in history. The second major idea concerns the New Testament teaching about divorce and remarriage. There is a universal memory of Jesus' teaching about divorce and remarriage, a memory articulated in the parabolic saying "everyone who divorces his wife and marries another commits adultery." There is also diverse interpretation of Jesus' parable by Mark, Matthew and Paul, and exceptions allowed by Matthew for *porneia* and by Paul in the case that came to be known in history as the Pauline Privilege. Over its long history, the Catholic Church has dissolved unquestionably valid marriages on the basis of either this Pauline Privilege, or its companion Petrine Privilege or nonconsummation. The minor idea concerns that process known as annulment, in which the Catholic Church declares that in a given relationship, thought to be a marriage, there never was at any time a valid marriage bond. Annulment, for one reason and another, has increased at an incredible rate in the dioceses of the United States over the past ten years.

Questions for Reflection

1. Given its evident historical practice, is it accurate to say that the Roman Catholic Church never grants divorces? In your judgment, is there any difference between the divorces granted by civil courts and the dissolutions granted by the Catholic Church? If there is, what is it?

2. Can you articulate clearly the difference between the dissolution of marriage, by use of the Pauline Privilege, for instance, and an annulment? Do you see a dissolution and an annulment as truly different?

3. If a marriage is thought to establish a blood relationship, as was the case in Jesus' culture, how could it be dissolved? Do you believe that marriage establishes a blood relationship? If you do not, how then does Jesus' saying about divorce and remarriage apply to you?

4. What was your reaction when you read that the saying of Jesus about divorce and remarriage "has to be a parable"? If it is a parable, and not a law for instance, what difference would it make? If it is not a parable, which of the New Testament versions of it should the Catholic Church choose to follow? Why?

5. What is your reaction to the practice of the Orthodox Churches toward the innocent party in a divorce proceedings? Does that practice, in your opinion, have anything to offer to the pastoral practice of the Catholic Church in the twentieth century? What do you think should be the attitude of the Church to those who have been divorced and remarried while their original spouse is still alive?

NOTES

1. Bruce J. Malina, *The New Testament World: Insights from Cultural Anthropology* (Atlanta: John Knox, 1981) 102-103.

2. Ibid., 104.

3. Those who wish to survey the opinions may consult J. Fitzmyer, "The Matthean Divorce Texts and Some New Palestinian Evidence," *TS* 37 (1976) 197-226, and A. Myre, "Dix ans d'exegese sur le divorce dans le Nouveau Testament," *Le Divorce* (Montreal: Fides, 1973).

4. Quentin Quesnell, "Made Themselves Eunuchs for the Kingdom of Heaven," *Catholic Biblical Quarterly* 30 (1968) 349.

5. Bruce J. Malina, *The New Testament World* 118-121.

6. Theodore Mackin, *Divorce and Remarriage* (New York: Paulist, 1984) 86.

7. *The Apostolic Fathers,* trans. Francis X. Glimm et al. (Washington: Catholic University of America Press, 1962) 264.

8. PG 31,849 and 852.

9. PG 32, 678-679.

10. PG 32,804-805.

11. PL 26,135.

12. PL 26,135.

13. PL 22,562.

14. PL 40,455.

15. PL 34,1253.

16. PL 40,378.

17. PL 40,378-379.

18. PL 40,388.

19. PL 187,1407.

20. PL 192,919.

21. *Tablet* (February 14, 1987) 177.

6

The Sacrament of Marriage: Disputed Questions

Embodied Love

In chapter 1 I briefly analyzed friendship and love. In chapter 2 I argued that the mutual love of husband and wife, and their desire to be best friends forever, is of the essence of both marriage and the sacrament of marriage. In chapter 3 I sketched the nature of love in a Christian marriage as neighbor-love which is giving-way, mutual service and faithful. In this section I discuss marital love yet again, this time as it is embodied in sexuality and sexual intercourse. This question is of central concern to Christian marriage, if only because the Christian tradition has shown, and continues to show an essential ambivalence toward sexuality and intercourse which many Christians have absorbed as an essential negativity. What is said here is said consciously as *reverse discrimination* to right the negative imbalance of the tradition with a more positive approach.

Earlier we dealt with the general ambivalence of the western tradition toward the body and sexuality. Feminist theologians have pointed out recently that there is an even greater ambivalence in the tradition toward the female body and female sexuality, which is seen as a source of temptation and sin to celibate males.[1] That ambivalence continues in modern Catholic theology as a spiritualizing approach to sexuality and sexual intercourse in marriage. That approach locates the principal value of human sexuality and intercourse exclusively on the spiritual level of human existence, a level judged to be superior to the bodily.

The objection I have to the spiritualizing approach is well articulated by Milhaven: "Man does do these spiritual, personal things in his sexual life (encounters, communicates, expresses love, etc.), and they do constitute the principal value of human sexuality, but not solely. The bodiliness and the sexualness with which he does them changes intrinsically their nature and therefore their value from what they would be in a nonbodied, nonsexual person's life."[2] The encounter, the interpersonal communication, the love-making between a man and a woman, indeed between any two human beings, are essentially embodied activities. The integrated human self, as distinct from the dichotomous body-soul self, is essentially a body-self. The body grounds every human relationship in and to the world; the body can never be banished from the human. To attempt to spiritualize human sexuality out of its bodiliness is as untrue to real human nature as the effort to reduce it to the merely animal.

It is not difficult to understand the mainspring of the spiritualizing tactic. Scorned bodiliness, always distrusted as sinful, and specifically the embodiedness of human sexuality and sexual intercourse, is precisely what led Augustine to declare the sin-corrupted body "burdensome to the soul."[3] That inherited distrust of the body has conditioned Christians to doubt the goodness of their sexuality and the goodness of sexual intercourse even between a husband and a wife. The loving communion of Will and Willma in marriage, however, and the sacramentality which is grounded in it, is a communion not only of spirit-selves but also, and essentially, of body-selves. Marital love is *agape*, the love of the spouse for the spouse's sake, but it is also more than *agape*. It is also *philia*, the love of the spouse as a friend; and it is also *eros*, the love of the spouse for one's own sake. These assertions must now be explicated.

Christian marital love, as we have highlighted several times, is a species of neighbor-love. Christian spouses, like all Christians, are subject to the great commandment to "love your neighbor (spouse) as yourself" (Mark 12:21). Since Augustine, that commandment has been interpreted in the Catholic tradition as grounding a wholly legitimate self-love. Though marital love is never exclusively self-love, it is unquestionably in part self-love, which comes to be grounded in neighbor-love in genuine communion. In the life-long communion which is marriage, Will and Willma come to value one another as full and fully esteemed partners, never as less than equal partners, and certainly never as objects to be used or abused, for one's own benefit. In such marital communion, "I love you" grows into "I love me and you" and, eventually, as Milhaven puts it so beautifully, into "we love us."[4] Though I do not wish to deal with this question here, I do wish to state that one of the reasons many men and women, including many Christian men and women, have difficulty coming to love another human being is that they have great difficulty coming to love themselves.

With self-love solidly grounded in neighbor-love, we can now consider *eros*, that rambunctious, irrational and selfish component of human love. The spiritualizers always want to transform it into *agape*. There is, however, no alchemy to effect such a transformation; *eros* is an essential, and therefore inescapable, element of human, embodied love. What humans can do in mutuality is to embrace it, to ground it and to give it distinctively human form. That distinctive form appears, I submit, when embodied *eros* is allied to the grace and wisdom of *agape*. When *eros* dominates, there is never mutuality and equality; there is only the selfish drive to dominate and to use, which is in effect to abuse another as a means to my own ends. That approach creates exactly what it seeks to avoid, isolation, alienation, loneliness, emptiness, everything but communion. When *agape* dominates, Will and Willma recognize that the other's well-being is the only way to their common well-being and, therefore, to each's individual well-being. When *agape* and *eros* are allies, spouses seek their mutual well-being as spouses and as a couple, in a love that is always embodied even when those things that fuel *eros*—youth, beauty, grace, health—have long since passed away.[5]

The Catholic doctrinal tradition, influenced as it is so strongly by Neo-Platonic philosophy, teaches that the more a created reality attains to the end for which it was created the truer and more moral it is. I am applying that doctrinal tradition here to *eros* and to sexual intercourse in marriage, and I am applying it sacramentally. *Eros*, sexuality and marital intercourse are all sacramental, not because of any human meaning assigned to them but simply because they are from God. They are God's created gifts to 'adam, Will and Willma, and they are good gifts. To use them as good gifts to make love and communion in Christian marriage (and that is explicitly the only use I am considering here) is to use them in a way that points to their origin in God. That is already to use them sacramentally, as outward signs of the presence of the God who is grace.

In a truly Christian marriage, therefore, there is no need to be afraid of graced *eros* and sexual intercourse; there is no need to spiritualize them; there is certainly no need to abstain from communion in the Body of Christ because of them (as was once the widespread case). For concrete men and women, each of whom is a body-self, entering into marital communion includes essentially, though not exclusively, body union. This marital communion of bodies, even in its most passionately erotic form, is an element in the embodied sacrament of marriage, it is graced, for it makes explicit and celebrates in the representation of God's gift the presence of the God who is Giver. Bodily union is far from all there is to marital communion, but bodily union occupies a central place in a Christian marriage as symbol of the communion, not only between Will and Willma, but also between humanity and God, who does not shrink from expressing his love for his people in that most beautiful and sexual of love songs, the Song of Songs.

The Song has always posed difficulties for Jewish and Christian interpretation, specifically the difficulty of deciding whether it was a paean to divine or to human love. For centuries, unwilling to admit that erotic love could have any place in their sacred writings, commentators opted for an allegorical reading. The Song of Songs, they piously and prudishly explained, was about divine love. But embodied men and women need only listen to the extraordinarily explicit words of erotic love to know otherwise.

"I am sick with love," the woman exclaims (2:5; 5:8). "Come to me," she cries out in desire for her lover, "like a gazelle, like a young stag upon the mountains where spices grow" (2:17; 8:14). When he comes, and gazes upon her nakedness, he is moved to ecstasy. "Your rounded thighs are like jewels, the work of a master hand. Your vulva is a rounded bowl that never lacks wine. Your belly is a heap of wheat encircled with lilies. Your two breasts are like fawns, twins of a gazelle. . . . You are stately as a palm tree, and your breasts are like its clusters. I say I will climb the palm tree and lay hold of its branches" (7:1-8). Her reply is not coy but direct. "I am my beloved's and his desire is for me. Come, my beloved, let us go forth into the fields. . . . There I will give you my love" (7:10-12). No woman or man who has ever been sick with love and desire can doubt the language or its intent.

Such explicitly erotic language has always cast doubts on the claim that the Song is clearly about divine love. A growing consensus has emerged today that the meaning of the Song is its literal meaning, and that its literal meaning is the one enshrined in any human love song. The Song may be an allegory about divine love, but only secondarily; it may be about non-sexual, spiritual love, but only derivatively. It is primarily and directly about erotic love, about love that at least includes *eros*, about love that is deliriously sick with passion and desire. It is about the love of *'adam*, Will and Willma, who in love seek the embodied presence of the other. This love is celebrated as gift, and therefore as symbol, of the God who loves humanity as Will and Willma love one another. It is celebrated, therefore, as good, to honor not only the Giver but also the gift, and *'adam* who uses the gift to make both human and, in representation, divine love. It is as intentional and explicit symbol that *eros* and sexual intercourse serve as outward signs, as sacraments, of the God who is grace and gracious.

Fruitfulness in Marriage

The prime challenge of the marriage of Will and Willma, and of every other marriage too, is the challenge to grow into marital communion. That challenge is the challenge to share themselves one with the other, the challenge "to move with integrity from I to we,"[6] from "I love you" to "we love us." It is the challenge to become, as we heard Doms suggest in an earlier chapter, a two-in-oneness. That becoming a we, a two-in-oneness, is the primary fruitfulness of marriage, and it is that fruitfulness which is the focus of this brief section.

The fruitfulness of marriage is not a new concern. The traditional discussion about the ends of marriage, which we considered in Chapter Four, is in reality a discussion about fruitfulness. That discussion enthroned the procreation of children as the primary fruitfulness of marriage and the mutuality of the spouses as a secondary fruitfulness. Though that hierarchy was understandable at a time when marriage was viewed exclusively as a social institution, it ceased to be understandable, or acceptable, when the social institution came to be viewed primarily as an interpersonal relationship. This adjustment in the understanding of marriage led, as we saw, to a corresponding adjustment in the arrangement of its ends by the Second Vatican Council, which set forth the mutuality of the spouses and the procreation of children as equal ends (GS 50; cf. Can. 1055, 1). I propose here to consider the fruitfulness of sacramental marriage under these two traditional headings, and add a third, namely, Christian life.

Fruitfulness is not a bedrock quality of marriage, for it depends on another quality, generativity, which is the capacity to generate and nurture life beyond oneself. It appears beyond doubt that the first life generated by the marriage of Will and Willma is their life together, what I have consistently called their mutual communion. That loving communion is a prime end of their marriage, indeed the reason they decided to get married in the first place. It is also a prime end of their sexual intercourse, for in every loving act of intercourse (and sadly, there are nonloving acts of intercourse, even in marriage) the communion of the spouses is both signified and enhanced. That fact is enshrined in the common phrase which describes their intercourse as "making love." Childless marriages are still fruitful marriages, made fruitful by the life of communion between the spouses generated and nurtured in them. As the Second Vatican Council taught, "marriage and conjugal love are by their nature ordained toward the begetting and educating of children," but that does not make "the other purposes of marriage of less account" (GS 50). The generation and the loving nurture of children frequently enhances the life of communion between the spouses, but if there is communion generated and nurtured between them—mutual love, mutual care, mutual concern, mutual joy, mutual enhancement of life—their marriage is already immensely fruitful even if childless.

The claim of the Vatican Council that "children are really the supreme gift of marriage and contribute very substantially to the welfare of their parents" (GS 50) will not be disputed by the majority of parents. We need not, therefore, spend much time establishing the generation of children as an important aspect of the fruitfulness of marriage. We do, however, need to spend some time highlighting the fact that the generativity, and fruitfulness, of marriage are not exhausted by the biological generation of children. To be generative and fruitful requires more than the simple act of biological intercourse. It requires also, and above all, the loving nurture of the life procreated in such intercourse. Will and Willma should realize that, for most parents, the nurture of that new personal life is more arduous and time-demanding than its procreation. They should realize that nurturing the child they have procreated, respecting and celebrating and shaping its individual freedom and life-direction, is the truly generative and difficult moment of parenthood. As any wise woman might advise them, they require a license more for parenting than for marriage.

The marriage of Will and Willma is not just any interpersonal relationship or any social institution, it is also a relationship, an institution and a marriage which is a Christian sacrament. Their marital communion, they say, is a sacrament of the holy communion between God and God's people and Christ and Christ's Church. They are called, therefore, to generativity and to fruitfulness, to enliven and to nurture, beyond the bounds of themselves and their family, and they are called to that generativity and fruitfulness in imitation of the Christ whom they confess as Lord.

Though biologically childless, the Christ was enormously fruitful, generating and nurturing all of those who are called by the name of Christian. He nurtured us to call upon God as *Abba*-Father (Mark 14:36) and, therefore, to view all men and women as our brothers and sisters. He summoned us to neighbor-love of these brothers and sisters. To be fruitful in their marriage in imitation of this Christ, to nurture their marriage as *Christian* marriage, Will and Willma must enliven and nurture life beyond the confines of their narrow family. They must love and care for their neighbors, they must live together joyously with their neighbors, they must enhance the lives of their neighbors as Christ sought to enhance them.

Parents frequently defend their every action by claiming that everything they do is "for the kids." There is something familially selfish about this attitude, something narrowly tunnel-visioned, something ultimately non-generative and non-fruitful, for if they leave to their children an unimproved world, what will they have ultimately done for them. The fruitfulness sought by Christ is a world of neighbor-love, a world in which neighbors enliven and nurture neighbors, a world of justice in which all children can be not only procreated but also personally nurtured in the love which gives life. To be fully generative and fruitful, Will and Willma will have to decide how they can enliven and nurture not only their mutual communion, not only their own children, but also the community in which they will pursue their communion and which they will leave to their children and their children's children. If their marriage is ever to become full sacrament, they will have to be fruitful in the third way as well as in the other two.

Indissoluble Marital Love and Indissoluble Marriage

In chapter 2 I sought to demonstrate that the matrix of the sacrament of Christian marriage, "the human conduct . . . that is taken and made into the sacrament,"[7] is the faith-informed love of the spouses. In this section, I continue the analysis of that matrix to illumine the question of the indissolubility of marriage, a question that continues to be hotly debated in the Christian Churches.

The marriage services of all the churches underscore the common Christian conviction that, when a man and a woman mutually covenant in Christian marriage, they commit themselves to abide in love and in covenant as long as life lasts. I share this common conviction. I take it to be self-evident that this is what both love and covenant mean. Love, by its very nature, tends to be lifelong; covenant, by its very nature, creates a free commitment in which I am honor-bound to keep my word. The question of indissolubility arises because many marriages do not last as long as life lasts; they end, they cease to be. The Churches are as divided on the proper approach to marriages that have ended, and to the remarriages which frequently follow them, as they are united in their conviction about the lifelong nature of marriage.

The Catholic moral tradition has long agreed that the obligation resulting from commitment is limited, not absolute, and that the commitment can be withdrawn and the obligation dispensed from for a reason accepted as greater than both. One example of the application of this principle is the fact that, though its reading of Jesus' saying on divorce and remarriage leads it to proclaim that "the essential properties of marriage are unity and indissolubility" (can. 1056), the Catholic Church dissolves some marriages it recognizes as valid. In plain language, it grants divorces under certain, clearly-specified circumstances. One such circumstance is the Pauline Privilege described in canon 1143, another the nonconsummation of marriage described in canon 1142.

A millennium of Catholic practice makes it clear that the only marriage the Church holds to be absolutely indissoluble is the marriage that is consummated as sacrament (cf. can. 1141). That long-standing practice clarifies something that is frequently ignored, namely, that indissolubility is not something given in a marriage but something only gradually acquired. In the Catholic tradition, again from a millennium of theory and practice, it is said to be acquired only when the spouses consummate their sacramental marriage. That consummation in turn, following the ancient Germanic tradition, is said to be achieved on the first act of marital intercourse.

Focusing for a moment on that traditional act of intercourse-consummation, we can say that, for most marriages, it happens soon after the wedding. For a significant number of marriages, however, many more than is commonly realized, consummation is postponed for some time, which means that those marriages remain dissoluble for some time. By paying attention to the shared experience of the married, Catholic theologians are learning a new fact today. They are learning that to claim that marital consummation takes place on the spouses' first act of sexual intercourse is overly romantic and unrealistic. They have learned from their tradition that the sacrament of marriage is what marriage is, and that marriage is rooted in the mutual love of the spouses. They are now learning from married people that the fullness of marital love is attained neither in a courtship, nor in a wedding ceremony, nor in a first act of marital intercourse. They are concluding from this fact that neither, therefore, is the fullness of a marriage, nor the sacrament of marriage, nor the indissolubility of a marriage attained.

The consummation of a marriage has little to do with one isolated act of sexual intercourse. Mackin expresses the experience of the married, I believe, when he states that to consummate a marriage means "to bring the marital relationship to its fullness."[8] A sacramental marriage, therefore, becomes consummated only when the marital love of the spouses reaches its fullness. Only when the mutual love of Will and Willma has reached such a level of fullness that they would not deliberately turn their back on it, nor on the marriage which is rooted in it, is their marriage consummated and, therefore, in practice indissoluble. To put it another way, in the terms of an earlier section, a sacramental marriage becomes indissoluble only when the marital love on which it is founded attains its practical fullness as communion that is mutually faithful and loyal, that is mutually giving way and that is mutually servant. Even sacramental marriage acquires indissolubility only when, and because, the marital love that grounds it has become faithful and indissoluble.

The fullness of Christian marital love is something to be acquired in a marriage. So too, therefore, is the marriage's indissolubility. In traditional theological language, love, marriage, sacrament of marriage and indissolubility are all equal and intertwined eschatological challenges, goals already-but-not-yet achieved. It is precisely this eschatological, ever-developing character of love, marriage and sacrament that makes Christian marriage such an excellent sign of the grace of God that is the love, covenant and communion between Christ and the ever-developing Church (LG,8,48).

Given the above, I am in complete agreement with a suggestion made by Mackin, namely, "that the words 'indissoluble' and 'indissolubility' be abandoned."[9] Indissolubility has been predicated traditionally as a quality or property of marriage (cf. Can. 1056), as something that exists "ontologically" apart from the will and the activity of the spouses. I do not believe that to be the case. If Christian marriage ever acquires the property of indissolubility, and remember it does actively acquire it rather than being given it automatically in a wedding ceremony, even in traditional Catholic theory and practice, it acquires it only from the love of the spouses becoming faithful and steadfast. Indissolubility becomes a property of Christian marriage only when and because steadfast fidelity becomes a property of Christian marital love.

The faithfulness of their marital love, and therefore the indissolubility of their marriage, is not independent of the partnered wills of Will and Willma, who are appropriately named. The fidelity of their love, and the consequent indissolubility of their marriage, is the result of their mutual decision not to turn their backs on their love and marriage. That decision is that their love and marriage are greater goods to them than either ending their love or transferring it to someone else. At that moment of mutual decision, their marriage is consummated and definitively acquires the properties of willed unity and willed indissolubility. That moment of decision, of course, will not be open to as clear a specification as the moment of their first sexual intercourse. There will be, therefore, an unclear sponginess in deciding when a marriage is consummated and, therefore, indissoluble. Clear or not, spongy or not, consummation as the spouses' conscious decision not to turn their backs on their marriage reflects the real experience of married couples better than consummation as their first, inexperienced act of sexual intercourse.

Divorce and Remarriage

The real history of marriages, of course, is that many which are never consummated as we have just explained consummation, cease to be and end in civil divorce. Many of those humanly unconsummated marriages are marriages between Roman Catholics, some thirty percent of which end in civil divorce. It is no secret that many of those civilly divorced Catholics contract second marriages, while their first spouses are still alive. Since these second marriages are held in Church law to be invalid, the spouses are prohibited from participating in the sacramental life of the Church. Many Catholic theologians, canon lawyers, ministers and lay people are asking today if the Church can do anything to minister to those in such second marriages. In May 1977 the Catholic bishops of the United States, the same body who had originally imposed the penalty, retroactively dropped the automatic excommunication for civilly divorced Catholics who remarry while their previous spouse is still alive. That was an apparently small, but in symbolic reality a momentous, gesture, for it removed a source of pain for many divorced and remarried Catholics. This section asks can anything more be done?

The breakdown of a marriage is always a human tragedy, causing pain to the spouses, their children, their family, their friends. When a marriage ends, within the very context in which they seek friendship, love, trust and security, many men and women find loneliness, hatred, distrust and insecurity. It is for this reason, for the hurt and the pain that it causes people, that divorce is an evil hated by God. We miss this point, and get the cart before the horse, when we think that divorce is evil because it is forbidden. Kelly points out, summoning Aquinas to his support, that "God is not offended by us except insofar as we harm ourselves and other people. Marriage breakdown and divorce is evil because of the human hurt and suffering caused by it. It offends God because people precious to him are being harmed and are hurting one another."[10]

We learned in the preceding chapter that the Catholic Church regularly dissolves marriages it holds to be valid. Those dissolutions are always on the basis of a good judged to be greater than the good of indissoluble marriage, for instance, the faith of one or both spouses or the salvation of their souls. In an address to the Roman Rota, the supreme marriage court of the Church, Pope Pius XII explained that "the supreme norm according to which the Roman Pontiff makes use of his vicarious power to dissolve a marriage is . . . the salvation of souls." He went on to point out that, in all of these decisions, "the common good of the religious society, and of human society in general, and the good of individuals find due and proportionate consideration."[11] Catholic theologians are asking today whether the good of divorced and remarried Catholics might find more proportionate consideration than it finds at present. They are also suggesting some possibilities.

First, there is the ancient practice of the Orthodox Church, going back to its great bishop-theologians Basil and John Chrysostom. That practice is governed by the principle of *oikonomia*, much weakened in its preempted English translation *economy*. *Oikonomia* refers to the order of salvation revealed in Christ. In that order, God is the benevolent and merciful father of the household (*oikos*); the Holy Spirit is the great comforter who makes every good possible in the household; Jesus is the good shepherd who, when necessary, leaves ninety-nine good sheep for a time to lead to salvation one that is lost; and the Church is the householder, merciful as the heavenly father of the household is merciful (Luke 6:36; Matt 5:44-48). *Oikonomia*, we must understand, is situated and flourishes in a context of gospel and grace, not of law. It heeds the gospel injunctions that "the law was given through Moses, grace and truth came through Jesus Christ" (John 1:17), and that "the written code kills, but the Spirit gives life" (2 Cor 3:6). *Oikonomia* cannot exist without great faith in the Spirit.

How does *oikonomia* touch the question about divorce and remarriage in the Catholic Church? While holding firmly to the belief that the gospel presents to Christians a demand for indissoluble marriage, the Orthodox Churches also acknowledge sadly that real men and women sometimes do not fully measure up to the gospel. They acknowledge that human marriages, even Christian marriages, die and that, when they are dead, it makes no sense to claim that they are still binding. When a marriage is dead, even when the spouses still live, *oikonomia* impels the householder-Church to be sad, yet also to be compassionate with the former spouses, even to the extent of permitting the remarriage of an innocent or a repentant spouse. The second marriage, however, is not on a par with the first, a fact which its liturgy makes clear.

There are prayers for the couple who, "being unable to bear the heat and burden of the day and the hot desires of the flesh, are now entering into the bond of a second marriage." There are petitions that they be pardoned for their transgressions, "for there is none sinless save only thou." Missing is the joy and glory of the first marriage; present is sorrow and repentance for its failure; present also is the necessary confession that no one in attendance, including the priest, is without sin. The economy of grace is constantly threatened by sin; Christian ideal is ever at the mercy of human frailty. It is in such an economy that the householder-Church is summoned to minister and to dispense compassion on behalf of the compassionate God.

What can the Roman Catholic Church learn from Orthodox *oikonomia*? Remember the Catholic Church has its own canonical procedures to dissolve valid marriages and to permit second marriages. Remember, too, that it has never condemned the Orthodox practice. Even the Council of Trent, which took a hard line on the question of indissolubility, worded its canon on indissolubility so as not to offend the Orthodox. It refused explicitly to declare that the practice of *oikonomia* did not have equal claim to the gospel tradition and to the name Christian.[12] Roman Catholic theologians are asking today if there is anything to be learned for the pastoral approach to divorce and remarriage from Orthodox *oikonomia*. The 1980 Synod of Bishops presented to Pope John Paul II a proposition asking that the Orthodox practice be carefully studied for any light it might shed on that pastoral approach.

It will never be a matter of simply importing the Orthodox practice lock, stock and barrel into the Catholic practice. Differentiations on the basis of different traditions will have to be made. In the present situation, however, and especially given the large numbers of Catholics involved in second marriages while their first spouses are still alive, there is at least a demand for pastoral discernment. The Catholic Church is being summoned to discern whether its traditional understanding of Jesus' words against divorce and remarriage precludes the development of an *oikonomia* approach to the pastoral care of its members in second marriages. Many of those marriages have become so stable and fruitful, and the families nurtured in them so Christian, that they cannot be abandoned without serious spiritual, emotional and economic harm to all involved.

There is strong support for reassessment in every sector of the Church, especially among women, who know that women frequently suffer most from divorce and remarriage.[13] The Church's theologians are doing what theologians are supposed to do, they are raising questions about traditional Christian faith and practice and their ongoing relationship to the Gospel. The specific question concerning the practice surrounding divorce and remarriage can be clearly stated. Can the Catholic Church continue to claim fidelity to the total economy revealed by the compassionate God and continue to permit one element in that economy, namely, its reading of Jesus' words on divorce and remarriage, to override all others? The question does not admit of an easy answer. But a Church faithful to the Gospel, and to the Comforter-Spirit who continues to reveal its meanings, can face it secure in the belief that the Spirit will lead it into the truth of God as surely today as yesterday.

Internal Forum

This section rightfully belongs as a second part of the preceding section but, given the importance and frightening lack of understanding of the theological principle and practice discussed here, I have decided to let it stand on its own. Despite the array of possibilities offered by ecclesiastical tribunals there are marriage cases which cannot be brought to judgment by a tribunal because some legal requirement is missing. To cite just one case. A young friend of mine, Bob I shall call him, had been married for seven years. To his sorrow, and with no apparent medical explanation, no children had been born in the marriage. One evening, out of the blue, Bob's wife told him that she was leaving him to marry another man. She also told him that the reason they had no children was that she had been aborting regularly during the marriage because she had never wanted children. It later transpired that, before their marriage, she had told two friends of her plan to do this. I explained to Bob that this was a solid case to submit to the local tribunal for an annulment of the marriage. When he tried to do so, he encountered a major legal obstacle, his wife and her friends refused to testify before the tribunal about her premarriage plan to abort any fetus. The tribunal was stymied, and the process ended without any resolution. An ancient Catholic safety valve, generally known as the internal forum solution, comes into play in this case.

When a case is settled in a marriage tribunal, it is said to be settled in the external forum, the forum of institutional law. But a long Catholic tradition insists that moral questions are not settled ultimately in the external forum, but in the internal forum of good conscience and good faith. As Fr. John Catoir, chief judge of an ecclesiastical tribunal for ten years, puts it: "In the past, Catholics were led to believe that the reward of heaven or the pain of hell was somehow related to the judgment of canon lawyers, but this is an incorrect understanding of revelation. A person's destiny before God is not necessarily based on his juridical standing in the Catholic church."[14] A long ethical tradition, recently underscored by the Second Vatican Council's Declaration on Religious Freedom, supports Catoir's judgment. How does it relate to Bob's case?

In good conscience Bob knows that his first "marriage" was a non-marriage, because his wife consented to it fraudulently; before the marriage, she had planned to defraud him of his children. He knows that were the tribunal process able to proceed to its legal completion, the "marriage" would be declared null, and he would be free to remarry. Suppose he meets someone else, falls in love with her and marries her while his first "spouse" is still alive; two questions of importance to him arise. Is his second marriage a valid marriage in the eyes of the Catholic Church, and can he and his wife continue to take Communion in the Church? The answer to both questions is a qualified yes.

In the external forum the second marriage cannot be considered valid because the first "marriage" has never been annulled and, therefore, they cannot share Communion in the Church. In the personally and morally more crucial internal forum, however, as long as Bob and his new wife have married with an honest and conscientious decision that they are free to marry, the Church can and does accept their decision of conscience, cannot and does not consider them sinners, and cannot and does not bar them from full union in the sacramental life of the Church. To reach such a conscientious, internal forum decision, they should seek the counsel of a priest. The moral bottom line, however, is not the priest's counsel but their honest decision of conscience that they are free to marry and free, therefore, to take Communion in the Church.

An internal-forum solution, it should be understood, cannot be applied indiscriminately in every difficult marriage case, but only after serious consideration of an individual case. In those cases in which it can be applied, certain conditions enter into or are attached to the decisions. The following are always enumerated. First, none of the present canonical solutions can be applied to the case. Second, the first marriage must be irretrievably ended and reconciliation impossible; an uncontested divorce, refusal of one party to be reconciled, obligations toward children in the second marriage may be taken as signs of this. Third, obligations deriving from a first marriage must be fully accepted and discharged; reasonable child support and alimony, equitable property settlement, acceptance of any responsibility for the failure of a first marriage and sorrow for any personal sin in that failure are among such obligations. Fourth, obligations deriving from the second marriage must be responsibly accepted and discharged, and the spouses in the second marriage must demonstrate that they intend to live in a stable marriage in a church community; the birth of children, the stability of the second marriage over a period of years, the genuine desire to participate in the full life of the Church may be taken as signs of such sincere responsibility. Fifth, the desire for the sacraments must be motivated by genuine Christian faith, the presence of which may be presumed in those who are sincerely pained by being barred from normal participation in the sacraments.

Catoir sums up succinctly the Church's position on internal forum. If Bob "had good reason to suspect the validity of the first marriage, I believe I would have a moral obligation to support his conscience."[15] That summary judgment may stand as clear conclusion to this section.

Ecumenical Marriage

Though it is not a marriage between two baptized believing Catholics, as is the marriage of Will and Willma, there is another kind of sacramental marriage which we must briefly consider, namely, the marriage of a believing Catholic and a believing member of another Christian tradition. In 1981, researchers Hoge and Ferry reported that 40 percent of Catholics who marry, marry someone of another Christian tradition.[16] Most commentators agree that, in 1993, the number is closer to 50 percent and growing. These facts ought not to come as a surprise to us. Given the educational, economic and social mobility of the populations in America, it is entirely predictable that men and women of different Christian faiths will meet, fall in love and marry in ever growing numbers. The sheer force of the numbers, however, demand a concerted pastoral strategy from the churches.

Traditionally such marriages have been called "mixed marriages," and have been viewed negatively by the Christian Churches. The 1917 *Code of Canon Law*, for instance, encapsulated the attitude of the Roman Catholic Church. "The church everywhere most severely prohibits the marriage between two baptized persons, one of whom is a Catholic, the other of whom belongs to a heretical or schismatic sect. If there exists the danger of perversion of the Catholic spouse or child, the marriage is forbidden even by divine law" (Can. 1060). Clearly, a mixed marriage was a dangerous evil, and the only safe way to deal with it was to avoid it.

The corresponding canon in the 1983 *Code* signals an important change in attitude. "Without the express permission of the competent authority, marriage is prohibited between two baptized persons, one of whom was baptized in the Catholic Church or received into it after baptism and has not defected from it by a formal act, the other of whom belongs to a church or ecclesial community not in full communion with the Catholic Church" (Can. 1124). Gone are the negative tones, and the harsh descriptions of the nonCatholic as heretic or schismatic. They have been replaced with positive approval of the nonCatholic's baptism and membership within a Christian Church, an approval which reflects the Second Vatican Council's momentous admission that there are other Christian Churches besides the Catholic Church and other followers of Christ besides Catholics. That changed ecclesiological climate is reflected in a changed attitude toward mixed marriages. To underscore that changed climate and attitude, I have explicitly rejected the term "mixed marriage," along with its negative nuances, and have replaced it with the term "ecumenical marriage."[17] This section seeks to explore briefly some implications of this change of climate and of term.

The word "ecumenical" invokes a context larger than marriage. It derives from the Greek *oikumene*, the whole inhabited world; it refers, in contemporary Christian usage, to the search of the Churches for worldwide unity and communion. The phrase "ecumenical movement" describes activities designed to promote that communion. My phrase "ecumenical marriage" is to be understood in this broader context. The phrase, however, requires careful definition and understanding, for not every marriage in which one spouse is said to be Catholic and the other is said to belong to another Christian tradition is, in my judgment, an ecumenical marriage.

There are, as I see it, three possibilities, specified by the faith or nonfaith of the prospective partners. There is the case in which neither partner believes in any Christian tradition, the case in which only one partner believes, and the case in which both partners are active believers. My term ecumenical marriage refers only to the third case, the case in which the spouses share a common Christian faith in one God, one Christ, one Spirit, one baptism. An ecumenical marriage is a marriage in which the spouses are mutually covenanted to grow together in that common faith, though each in good conscience is resolved to continue to belong to a different Christian Church.

In November 1970 the Catholic bishops of the United States issued instructions for the care of ecumenical marriages, in which they suggested that the efforts of ecumenical couples to achieve unity in faith are a participation in the broader efforts toward unity among the divided Christian Churches. Ten years later, in his important exhortation on the family, *Familiaris Consortio*, Pope John Paul II made the same point. "Marriages between Catholics and other baptized persons," he wrote, "contain numerous elements that could be made good use of, both for their intrinsic value and for the contribution they can make to the ecumenical movement." He supports my definition of an ecumenical marriage when he goes on to insist that "this is particularly true when both parties are faithful to their religious duties" (n. 78). I propose now to draw out from these positive assessments some pastoral implications for ecumenical marriages.

First, I invite all spouses in ecumenical marriages to look upon their marriages as neither evils nor sources of danger, but as opportunities and challenges. The challenge they offer to the spouses is twofold. There is, first, the challenge to grow together into the communion of the whole of life that is the challenge generally of every marriage; there is, second, the challenge to grow together into the communion of Christian faith, ecumenically differentiated though it be, that is the specific challenge of every Christian marriage. The communion of faith achieved by spouses in an ecumenical marriage has a double root. It is rooted, initially, in their shared baptismal covenant to become one in Christ; it is rooted, again, in their shared marital covenant to become one body-person (Gen 2:24). The loving communion many ecumenical spouses achieve out of this twin root far exceeds the communion achieved between their Churches, even the communion achieved in most Christian congregations. Exemplified in loving reconciliation, healing of divisions, mutual trust and respect, it is a gift for them and a challenge to their Churches to imitate.

Second, I invite all Christian spouses to recognize the context of grace in which their marriage places them. For Catholic spouses, that ought to be easy, for they are accustomed to hearing that their marriages are sacraments, signs and instruments, of grace. For Protestant spouses, it may not be so easy, for their Churches normally do not acknowledge marriage as sacrament. They do, however, think of it as a covenant, modeled upon and therefore sign of the covenant between Christ and his Church. When an ecumenical family lives a life that is obviously covenantal, it becomes both a sign and an instrument of the presence of Christ and the God he reveals. That presence, of course, is precisely what the Christian tradition intends in the word *grace*. Because Christian marriages are signs and instruments of grace, everything the spouses do lovingly in them, their mutual trust, respect, service, love, including sexual love, places them in the presence of the God who is grace, and makes them holy. That ecumenical spouses see their marriage as not just a social but also a religious reality offers them yet one more fertile base on which to nurture their mutual communion.

Third, I invite all ecumenical spouses, indeed all Christians, to seek without prejudice to understand one another's beliefs. In the case of ecumenical spouses, the effort to love one another totally embraces the need to love one another precisely *as* Catholic or *as* Lutheran. That need will be satisfied more easily the more each spouse understands the faith of the other. Though the Catholic Church still requires that the Catholic spouse in an ecumenical marriage promise to do all that is in her or his power to ensure that children are raised as Catholics, it also has no doubt that the education of the children in the marriage is the mutual responsibility of both parents. The faith of both parents, and specifically the depth of their understanding of it, is always a critical factor in the religious education of the children. Both parents in an ecumenical marriage must strive to understand as fully as possible the faith each brings to the marriage. When each understands both faiths, the divisive procedure of the children consulting one parent for information on one faith and the other parent for information on the other is precluded.

Fourth, I invite ecumenical spouses, and again all Christians, to recognize without defensiveness that ecumenical families should, at least occasionally, worship God together. A now traditional Christian adage is especially true in ecumenical families: the family that prays together stays together. It is not enough that their private family prayer be together. Their public worship, the communal commemoration of Jesus the Christ, should also be together on a regular basis, and it should include, at least on special occasions, the sharing of Communion if they so desire. This question of shared communion is one that is hotly, and emotionally, debated in and between the Christian Churches, and the plan of this book does not permit me to treat of it adequately here.[18] Here I content myself merely by submitting that the spiritual need of ecumenical couples is frequently serious enough for their two Churches to respond to them pastorally by offering them the Christian hospitality of shared Communion.

Finally, I invite ecumenical spouses, and all Christians, to remember the self-definition of our common Lord, the one who came "not to be served but to serve" (Mark 10:45). No Christian family, ecumenical or not, can be anything less than a family of service. Christian spouses are called to be fruitful in a discipleship of service of one another, of their family, of their churches and of the communities in which they live. Ecumenical spouses are called to the specific service of other ecumenical families; they are called to share with them and to sustain them with their lived ecumenical resolve and insight. Their ecumenical service is one more gift and challenge ecumenical spouses offer to their divided churches, one more sign that Christians who differ can still work together in and for Christ, and for his great ecumenical goal "that they may all be one" (John 17:21).

The Minister of the Sacrament of Marriage

There remains one, brief section to complete this book. Because it is a book not about *marriage* but about the *sacrament of marriage*, we must consider the theological question of the minister of the sacrament. Two broadly based answers to the question stand in contrast. The traditional teaching of the Orthodox Churches is that the presiding priest is the sacramental minister, that of the Catholic Church that the couple are the ministers of the sacrament one to the other.

The teaching of the Catholic Church derives inescapably from its identification of the marriage contract with the sacrament. To the extent that the mutual consent of Will and Willma initiates their marriage, and to the extent that their marriage is also their sacrament, we may agree that they are co-ministers of the sacrament one to the other. However, if what I have argued throughout this book about the specificity of Christian marriage as sacrament of the communion between Christ and Christ's Church is correct, we may have to consider another co-minister. I submit that the law, which requires for the validity of a Christian marriage the presence of a priest or deacon of the Church, is a law requiring the presence of someone more than just a legal witness to the marriage, for the priest or deacon receives their covenant "in the name of the church" (Can. 1108).

In any marriage in the western world, as will be clear by now, a man and a woman consent to a loving partnership for the whole of life. In a Christian marriage they do the same, and more. They consent to live and to love not only as spouses but specifically as *Christian* spouses, making explicit and celebrating in their marital communion the covenantal communion between Christ and Christ's Church. That Church, therefore, has a stake in their marriage, a need to know whether these spouses can or are willing to represent its covenant with Christ, a need to enhance their readiness to do so. In some kind of pre-marriage inventory, therefore, it inquires into their talent/charism not just for marriage, but specifically for Christian marriage. The official presence of a minister of the Church at their wedding announces on behalf of the Church that, in the case of this couple, that talent/charism has been found.

The Church's minister, therefore, I submit, is present at a Christian marriage as more than a simple witness to the spousal consent. He is there also to perform a specific ministry in the name of the Church. He is there to confirm the couple's faith as the faith of the Church; absence of this faith, as we saw, nullifies the sacrament. He is there to attest to the presence in this couple of the talent/charism, not merely for marriage but specifically for Christian marriage. He is there to receive on behalf of the Church the couple's consent to live in loving partnership for the whole of life as representation of the irrevocable covenant between Christ and Christ's Church. He is there to commission the couple precisely to that task. He is there, finally, to bless the couple in the name of the Church, and therefore in the name of Christ and of God, and to promise them the Church's support in the lifelong fulfillment of their sacramental task.

The position which holds that *only* the couple are the ministers of the sacrament of marriage, and that the minister is *only* a witness, misses these ecclesial dimensions. It risks reducing Christian marriage to the same status as any other marriage, and it risks reducing it specifically to the status of a private matter between the couple. However much the couple would like their marriage to be merely a private matter between them, no marriage in the western world is such an exclusively private affair. Every marriage is also a *societal* affair and, therefore, must be conducted according to society's laws; every Christian marriage is also a *Church* affair and, therefore, must be conducted according to the Church's theological and canonical laws. I submit that the Church's minister is required to be present precisely to tend to, that is, to minister to, the Church's legitimate stake in a Christian marriage.

I do not intend to espouse, because I do not believe, the Orthodox position that the priest is the *sole* minister of Christian marriage. I do intend to espouse the position which sees the religious minister as more than a legal witness to the consent which initiates marriage, which sees him as a *co-minister* with the couple of the religious sacrament of marriage. In the social climate of the western world, with its emphasis on freedom and individuality, it needs to be emphasized that the Christian Church has as much stake in a Christian marriage as the marrying couple. The minister of the Church is designated to be present at their marriage to reveal and to minister to that stake.

Summary

This chapter explained four major ideas. First, the mutual love of spouses in a Christian marriage is essentially that kind of embodied love which has long been suspect in the Christian tradition. The love between spouses is never exclusively *agape*, a spiritual love, it is also *philia* and *eros*, love which is expressed and nurtured in bodily actions. It is not only with their spirits but also with their bodies that spouses make love and are sacraments of the gracious love of God. Second, generativity and fruitfulness in Christian marriage extend to more than the mere generation and nurture of children. They extend equally to the generation and nurture of a life of communion between the spouses and a life of Christian discipleship. Third, the human consummation of a marriage is attained, not in an isolated act of sexual intercourse but when the marital love of the spouses reaches such a fullness that they would not now deliberately turn their backs on it. When a marriage achieves such consummation, it also becomes absolutely indissoluble, a fact which has serious implications for the question of divorce and remarriage which so vexes the Catholic world today. Fourth, fueled by the statistic that one in every two Catholics who marry today marry someone of another Christian denomination, the chapter considered ecumenical marriage and the context of sacramental grace in which it situates the spouses.

Questions for Reflection

1. How do you feel about your sexuality and its use in marriage as a source of holiness? (This is one of the things the Catholic Church means when it teaches that marriage is a sacrament.)

2. Do you understand the implications of the Catholic teaching that sacramental marriage *becomes* indissoluble only when it is consummated? Does it make more sense to you to say that the consummation of a marriage takes place in the first spousal act of sexual intercourse or in the

fullness of the loving relationship between the spouses? What implications do you see in either position for the marriage of Will and Willma?

3. What do you understand about the Orthodox practice of *oikonomia*? Does the Catholic Church, in your judgment, have anything to learn from that practice?

4. Are you comfortable with the claim that a Christian marriage, such as that between Will and Willma, is a matter for the whole Church and not just for the couple? Why? Does it make more sense to you to say that the presiding priest or deacon is merely a witness of marriage or to say that he is also a co-minister of the sacrament with the couple?

5. Now that you have completed this book, list and explain five things that you have learned that will make a difference in your Christian marriage.

NOTES

1. See Rosemary Radford Ruether, *New Woman/New Earth: Sexist Ideologies and Human Liberation* (New York: Seabury, 1975) esp. 186–211, and *Sexism and God-Talk: Toward a Feminist Theology* (Boston: Beacon, 1983) esp.179–192.

2. "Conjugal Sexual Love and Contemporary Moral Theology," TS 35 (1974) n. 15, 700.

3. *City of God* 13, 16.

4. "Conjugal Sexual Love" 705.

5. The ideas expressed here on *eros* and *agape* were stimulated by Helmut Gollwitzer's beautiful book, *Song of Love: A Biblical Understanding of Sex* (Philadelphia: Fortress, 1979).

6. Evelyn E. Whitehead and James D. Whitehead, *Marrying Well: Stages on the Journey of Christian Marriage* (New York: Image Books, 1983) 234.

7. Mackin, *The Marital Sacrament* 11.

8. Ibid., 674.

9. "The International Theological Commission and Indissolubility," William P. Roberts, ed., *Divorce and Remarriage: Religious and Psychological Perspectives* (Kansas City: Sheed and Ward, 1990) 59.

10. Kevin T. Kelly, *Divorce and Second Marriage: Facing the Challenge* (New York: Seabury, 1983) 39.

11. AAS 43 (1941) 425–426.

12. See DS 1807 and footnote. See also Kelly, *Divorce and Second Marriage,* 87–88.

13. See the statistics reported in *Time* (June 22, 1992) 64–65.

14. John T. Catoir, *Catholics and Broken Marriage: Pastoral Possibilities of Annulment, Dissolution, the Internal Forum* (Notre Dame: Ave Maria Press, 1979) 51.

15. Ibid., 57–58.

16. Dean Hoge and Kathleen M. Ferry, *Empirical Research on Interfaith Marriage in America* (Washington: United States Catholic Conference, 1981) 1.

17. See Michael G. Lawler, *Ecumenical Marriage and Remarriage: Gifts and Challenges to the Churches* (Mystic: Twenty-Third Publications, 1990).

18. Those who are interested in pursuing the question can consult my treatment of it in *Ecumenical Marriage and Remarriage,* 86–92. See also the important "Directory for the Application of Principles and Norms on Ecumenism" issued by the Pontifical Council for Promoting Christian Unity in March, 1983: *Origins* 23 (1993) 129–160.

Bibliography

Achtemeier, Elizabeth R. *The Committed Marriage*. Philadelphia: Westminster, 1976.

Barth, Markus. *Ephesians*. New York: Doubleday, 1974.

Basset, William and Peter Huizing. *The Future of Christian Marriage*. New York: Herder, 1973.

Catoir, John T. *Catholics and Broken Marriage: Pastoral Possibilities of Annulment, Dissolution, the Internal Forum*. Notre Dame: Ave Maria Press, 1979.

Cooke, Bernard. *Sacraments and Sacramentality*. Mystic: Twenty-Third Publications, 1983.

Cuenin, Walter. *The Marriage of Baptized Non-Believers*. Rome: Gregorian University Press, 1977.

Dominian, Jack. *Christian Marriage*. London: Darton, Longman and Todd, 1968.

Dominian, Jack. *Marriage, Faith and Love*. New York: Crossroad, 1982.

Doyle, Thomas P., ed. *Marriage Studies: Reflections in Canon Law and Theology*, Vol. 2. Washington: The Catholic University of America Press, 1982.

Doyle, Thomas P., ed. *Marriage Studies: Reflections in Canon Law and Theology*, Vol. 3. Washington: The Catholic University of America Press, 1984.

Denneny, Raymond, ed. *Christian Married Love*. San Francisco: Ignatius Press, 1981.

Falk, Marcia. *Love Lyrics from the Bible: A Translation and Literary Study of the Song of Songs*. Sheffield: Almond Press, 1982.

Gollwitzer, Helmut. *Song of Love: A Biblical Understanding of Sex*. Philadelphia: Fortress, 1979.

Haring, Bernard. *No Way Out?: Pastoral Care of the Divorced and Remarried*. Slough, England: St. Paul Publications, 1990.

Haughton, Rosemary. *The Theology of Marriage*. Notre Dame: Fides, 1971.

Joyce, G. H. *Christian Marriage: An Historical and Doctrinal Study*. London: Sheed and Ward, 1933.

Kasper, Walter. *Theology of Christian Marriage*. New York: Crossroad, 1981.

Kelly, Kevin. *Divorce and Second Marriage: Facing the Challenge.* New York: Seabury, 1983.

Kennedy, Eugene. *What a Modern Catholic Believes about Marriage.* Chicago: Thomas More, 1972.

Kilcourse, George. *Double Belonging: Interchurch Families and Christian Unity.* New York: Paulist, 1992.

Lawler, Michael G. *Ecumenical Marriage and Remarriage: Gifts and Challenges to the Churches.* Mystic: Twenty-Third Publications, 1990.

Lawler, Michael G. *Symbol and Sacrament: A Contemporary Sacramental Theology.* New York: Paulist, 1987.

Mackin, Theodore. *What is Marriage?* New York: Paulist, 1982.

Mackin, Theodore. *Divorce and Remarriage.* New York: Paulist, 1984.

Mackin, Theodore. *The Marital Sacrament.* New York: Paulist, 1989.

Malone, Richard, and John R. Connery, eds. *Contemporary Perspectives on Christian Marriage.* Chicago: Loyola University Press, 1984.

Meyendorff, John. *Marriage: An Orthodox Perspective.* New York: St. Vladimir's Seminary Press, 1978.

Nelson, James B. *Embodiment: An Approach to Sexuality and Christian Theology.* Minneapolis: Augsburg, 1978.

Roberts, William P. *Divorce and Remarriage: Religious and Psychological Perspectives.* Kansas City: Sheed and Ward, 1990.

Roberts, William P. *Marriage: Sacrament of Hope and Challenge.* Cincinnati: St. Anthony Messenger Press, 1983.

Schillebeeckx, Edward. *Marriage: Secular Reality and Saving Mystery.* New York: Sheed and Ward, 1965.

Tetlow, Elizabeth M., and Louis M. Tetlow. *Partners in Service: Towards a Biblical Theology of Christian Marriage.* Lanham: University Press of America, 1983.

Whitehead, Evelyn E., and James D. Whitehead. *A Sense of Sexuality: Christian Love and Intimacy.* New York: Doubleday, 1989.

Whitehead, Evelyn E., and James D. Whitehead. *Marrying Well: Stages on the Journey of Christian Marriage.* New York: Doubleday, 1983.

Young, James J. *Divorcing, Believing, Belonging.* New York: Paulist, 1984.

Young, James J., ed. *Ministering to the Divorced Catholics.* New York: Paulist, 1979.

General Index

'*adam*, 21, 37
annulment, 94–95
antinomianism, 53
Aquinas, xi, 4, 26, 28, 31, 60–62
Aristotle, 1, 4
Augustine, xi, 27, 29, 56–60, 88,
 99

Basil, 85, 107
body, 6, 21, 38
Body of Christ, 30, 44

Chrysostom, 86, 107
Cicero, 5
Clement of Alexandria, 54
concupiscence, 59
consent, 7, 63, 65, 67, 71
contract, 66
Council
 Florence, 63
 Lateran, 62
 Lyons, 63
 Trent, 63, 65, 108
 Vatican II, ix, 11, 19, 30, 70–71,
  84, 102, 112
 Verona, 63
covenant, 13, 20, 38
 marriage as, 13, 20–25, 114

disciple, 23
divorce
 and remarriage, 76, 85, 106–109

ecumenical marriage, 111–115
embodied love, 98–101
Ephesians, 21, 41–45

faith, 25–32
feminist theology, 13
friendship, 1–4
fruitfulness in marriage, 68,
 102–104

generativity, 102
Gnosticism, 53, 62
Gratian, 8, 64, 90

Hosea, 39

indissolubility, 49, 63, 64, 75, 90,
 104–106
intercommunion, 115
internal forum, 109–111

Jerome, 87
Justinian, ix, 8

love, 4–7, 19, 44, 47–49, 67, 68,
 70, 98–101

Manicheism, 57
marriage, 7–12
 and consent, 7, 63, 65, 67, 71
 and consummation, 64, 76, 90,
  94, 105